The Roman [illegible]
Shadwell, L[illegible]
a reappraisal

David Lakin, with Fiona Seeley, Joanna Bird,

Kevin Rielly and Charlotte Ainsley

MoLAS Archaeology Studies Series 8

Museum of London Archaeology Service

Published by the Museum of London Archaeology Service

A CIP catalogue record for this book is available from the British Library

Production and series design by Tracy Wellman
Typesetting and design by Jeannette van der Post
Reprographics by Andy Chopping
Copy editing by Katherine Barclay
Series editing by Sue Hirst/Susan M Wright

Printed by the Lavenham Press

Front cover: 2nd-century cremation burial in a pottery vessel covered with a pottery lid and accompanied by a 'poppyhead' beaker (<P5>–<P7>); detail on a decorated sherd of late 2nd-century samian ware pottery (<SAM39>); pair of Roman ceramic lamps (<S22>, <S21>); detail on a decorated sherd of 3rd-century samian ware pottery (<SAM62>)

The Roman tower at Shadwell, London: a reappraisal

MoLAS Archaeology Studies Series

1 A 14th-century pottery site in Kingston upon Thames, Surrey: excavations at 70–76 Eden Street, Pat Miller and Roy Stephenson
ISBN 1 901992 07 1

2 Excavations at 72–75 Cheapside/83–93 Queen Street, City of London, Julian Hill and Aidan Woodger
ISBN 1 901992 08 X

3 Bankside: excavations at Benbow House, Southwark, London SE1, Anthony Mackinder and Simon Blatherwick
ISBN 1 901992 12 8

4 A Romano-British cemetery on Watling Street: excavations at 165 Great Dover Street, Southwark, London, Anthony Mackinder
ISBN 1 901992 11 X

5 Excavations at 25 Cannon Street, City of London: from the Middle Bronze Age to the Great Fire, Nicholas J Elsden
ISBN 1 901992 22 5

6 The London Millennium Bridge: excavation of the medieval and later waterfronts at Peter's Hill, City of London, and Bankside, Southwark, Julian Ayre and Robin Wroe-Brown
ISBN 1 901992 25 X

7 An excavation in the western cemetery of Roman London: Atlantic House, City of London, Sadie Watson
ISBN 1 901992 26 8

8 The Roman tower at Shadwell, London: a reappraisal, David Lakin, with Fiona Seeley, Joanna Bird, Kevin Rielly and Charlotte Ainsley
ISBN 1 901992 27 6

CONTRIBUTORS

Principal author	David Lakin
Roman (non-samian) pottery	Fiona Seeley
Samian pottery	Joanna Bird
Samian potters' stamps	Brenda Dickinson
Roman glass	John Shepherd
Roman accessioned finds	Angela Wardle
Roman coins	Michael Hammerson
Roman leather	Carol van Driel-Murray
Animal bone	Kevin Rielly, Charlotte Ainsley
Graphics	Peter Hart-Allison, Julia Jarrett, Dorrie Orchard, Carol van Driel-Murray (leather), Eddie Jeffreys (samian ware)
Photography	Edwin Baker, Andy Chopping, Maggie Cox
Project managers	Richard Malt, Barney Sloane
Editors	David Bowsher, Susan M Wright, Peter Rowsome

CONTENTS

FIGURES

TABLES

SUMMARY

Excavations were undertaken between 1974 and 1976 in three areas (LD74, HIG74 and LD76) on the south side of The Highway, Shadwell, in the London borough of Tower Hamlets. Extensive archaeological remains of Roman and post-medieval date were uncovered during the course of the work, including the square base of a substantial Roman masonry structure (at LD74). This was interpreted by the excavator as a late 3rd-century military signal tower, on the basis of its form and its location and visibility on the north bank of the Thames, *c* 1.25km east of the main settlement at Londinium. Timber structures were found just to the east of the masonry building. Examination of the site archive has led to a reinterpretation of the site sequence, which included several phases of use from the 1st to late 4th century AD.

The site lay on Thames River Terrace gravels near a marked escarpment. Gravel and brickearth quarrying, in the late 1st or early 2nd century, was followed by the establishment of a cremation cemetery during the 2nd century, with nine cremations recorded in two clusters. The site lies *c* 500m east of the easternmost known extent of the main cemetery outside the Roman city, and 100m south of the projected line of a Roman road which ran through that cemetery. The 9m square masonry 'tower' is thought to date to the second half of the 2nd century or slightly later, and may, therefore, have been contemporary with, and a focus for, the burials. The method of construction of the 'tower', which had relatively shallow foundations, is consistent with that of mausolea, some of which are thought to have been tower-like in appearance.

In the 3rd century the area was divided into plots, first by fences and later by ditches and gullies, and a substantial, rectilinear, timber building and other structures and pits associated with domestic occupation, were established. Associated animal bone evidence may indicate that large-scale butchery took place nearby. In the mid 4th century, the latest phase of field boundaries was infilled and clay- and timber-lined tanks and drains constructed, suggesting that the site was turned over to industrial use. A pair of leather briefs was found in the fill of one of the tanks.

Demolition of the masonry structure, deposition of building rubble and the subsequent accumulation of agricultural soil marked abandonment of the area in the second half of the 4th century. Two inhumation burials may also date to this period, indicating a final return to use of the site as a cemetery.

The pottery and coin assemblages from Shadwell are unusually large for a non-urban site and follow an unusual chronological profile, peaking in the late 3rd century; a large farm or hinterland settlement perhaps lay nearby. There was little in the finds assemblage that could be characterised as military, except possibly the samian. The site produced some of the latest samian known from Britain, with a high proportion of late East Gaulish wares.

ACKNOWLEDGEMENTS

This publication is the product of a joint venture between English Heritage and the Museum of London Archaeology Service (MoLAS) to publish backlog sites identified in the London post-excavation review (DGLA 1989; see now Hinton and Thomas 1997). The research for this project was funded by English Heritage.

This publication would not have been possible without the persistence and enthusiasm of a large number of people, many of whom have contributed to this publication and whose names are listed above. In a project of this nature much rests on the, often unsung, work of the archivist and librarian. Thanks are, therefore, due to Cath Maloney and Alan Thompson (Museum of London), Nathalie Cohen (MoLAS) and the staff of the libraries of the Institute of Classical Studies and the Institute of Archaeology (University College London).

Thanks are also due to those readers at English Heritage and *Britannia*, in particular the editor of *Britannia*, Dr Lawrence Keppie, who commented on the academic content of the drafts of this study. The principal author of this report is grateful to David Bowsher and Bruno Barber for their comments on the cemetery sites and the potential relationship of those sites to the remains at Shadwell.

Thanks are due to Brian Kerr of English Heritage and to Gordon Malcolm and Barney Sloane (MoLAS) for management of the post-excavation programme. The summary was translated into French by Dominique de Moulins and into German by Friederike Hammer. The index was compiled by Susanne Atkin.

Joanna Bird would like to thank the following: Dr Dietwulf Baatz, Dr David Bird, Brenda Dickinson, B R Hartley, Dr Ingeborg Huld-Zetsche, Dr Klaus Kortüm, Geoff Marsh, Dr Allard Mees, the late Dr Ralph Merrifield, Harvey Sheldon, the late Dr Hans-Günther Simon and Dr Paul Tyers. A special debt is owed to the late Eddie Jeffreys (a volunteer) for his excellent drawings of the decorated samian.

Fiona Seeley would like to acknowledge Beth Richardson's work on the initial recording and quantifying of the Roman pottery and to thank her for her comments on the assemblage.

1 Introduction

1.1 Location and circumstances of fieldwork

The excavations at Shadwell took place in three stages, across two adjacent properties which lay on the south side of The Highway, Shadwell, London, E1, with an approximate centre at TQ 3488 8073, east of what is now Wapping Lane (Fig 1). The first site to be excavated (LD74) was directed by Tony Johnson on behalf of London and Middlesex Archaeological Society, and lay immediately east of 172–176 The Highway, London, E1. Initially three trial trenches were excavated, the westernmost of which was viewed to be the most promising and was expanded to allow an area excavation. Photographs taken after excavation at LD74 had ended suggest that not all of the archaeological features on this site were fully excavated. During the backfilling of this site a watching brief (HIG74) was undertaken by the newly formed Inner London Archaeological Unit (ILAU); the features noted during this work seem to have lain immediately to the south of LD74. The third site (LD76) lay in the plot to the east of LD74, where two of Johnson's trial trenches had been located, and was again excavated by ILAU. On both LD74 and LD76, initial clearance of modern overburden and intrusions had been made using mechanical means but all subsequent excavation was by hand. A total of more than 1300m^2 was excavated at the three sites.

The three sites were assessed together and form a single unit. The assessment, and the preliminary work which preceded it, demonstrated significant problems with the Shadwell archives, inevitably limiting the scope of subsequent work, so analysis was confined to the Roman sequences.

A preliminary phasing of the records from LD74 had been undertaken by 1977 and formed part of the undergraduate dissertation submitted by the excavator of the site (Johnson 1977). When the current programme of work commenced in 1995, the original site records for LD74 were not available and secondary sources of limited scope had to be used to establish a rough framework for the site sequence. Site records from HIG74 were entirely lacking and no reference could be found to any finds nor to post-excavation analysis of the records. Consequently HIG74 was omitted from further study.

The coins from sites LD74 and LD76 had been dated before the start of English Heritage funded work on this project. The samian pottery from both sites and the coarse wares from LD76 had also been studied prior to the current programme of work (Bird 1987, 328–9). The non-samian pottery from LD74 was not available to study. Only glass, of the other categories of finds, had been the subject of a completed finds report.

The analysis of these sites has had to be undertaken therefore largely from scratch using less than wholly satisfactory records. Despite this it has proved possible to establish a plausible sequence for the two sites for which records survive (LD76 and LD74). This in turn allowed the final stages of analysis of the available finds.

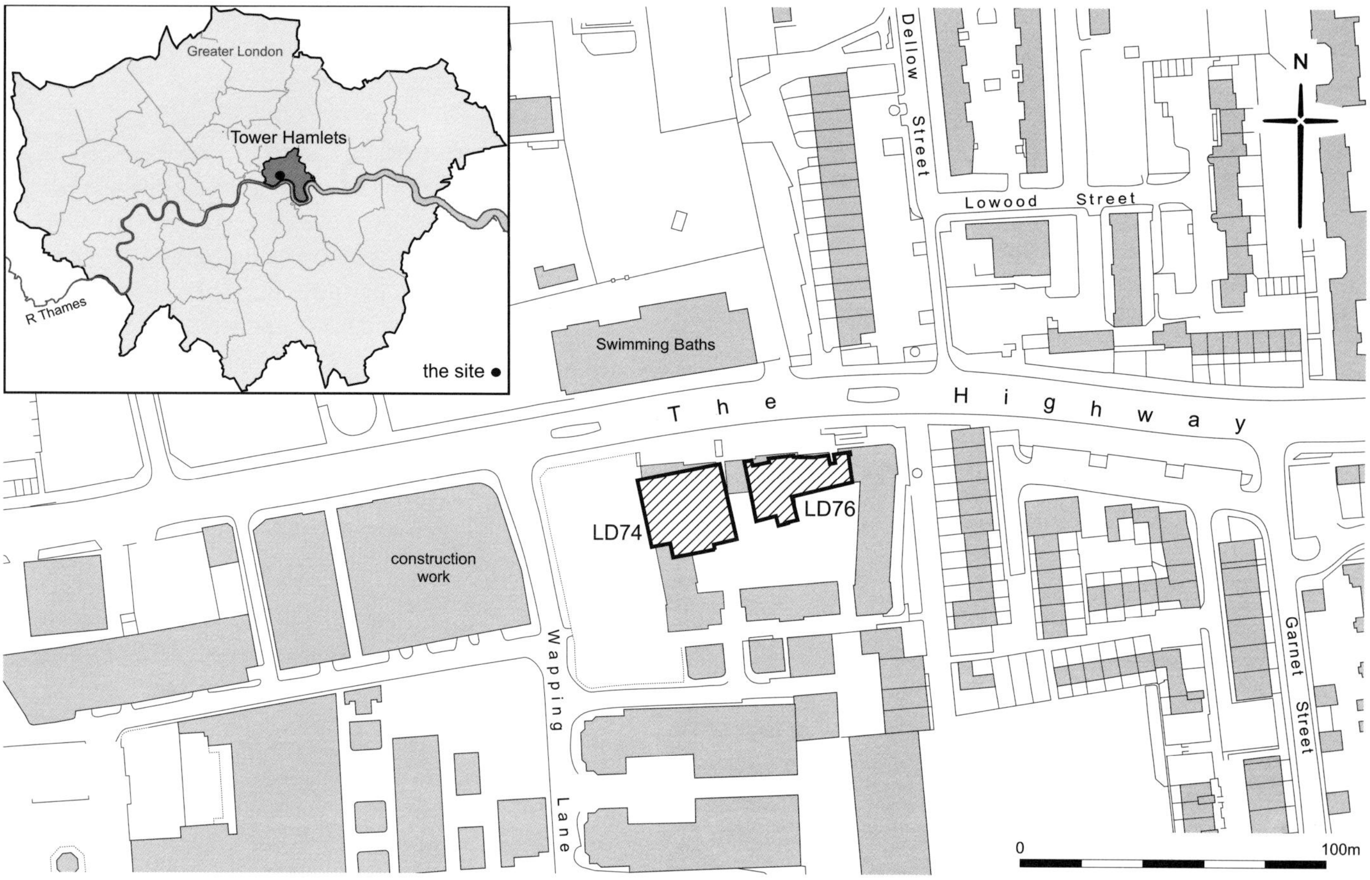

Fig 1 Site and trench location (scale 1:2500)

The records, finds and environmental samples for LD76 and certain finds from LD74 (samian, coins and animal bone) and their archive, and the detailed results of analysis for both LD74 and LD76 are in the Museum of London's London Archaeological Archive and Research Centre (LAARC) and may be consulted by prior arrangement.

1.2 Archaeological background

Evidence for prehistoric activity from the vicinity of the study area is very limited. Scattered remains of finds of Mesolithic to Bronze Age material have been found in the southern part of Tower Hamlets from The Minories in the west to Butcher Row, Ratcliff, in the east. Nearby excavations to the north have produced very small quantities of prehistoric material (Barber and Bowsher 2000, 50–1). None of these finds has been clearly indicative of prehistoric settlement anywhere nearby, although the recent discovery of Neolithic worked flints at 130–162 The Highway (CYD96, some 200m to the west) may alter this.

Few settlements have been identified in the hinterland of Roman London and fewer still have been the subject of extensive excavations (Bird, 1996). The site lies *c* 1.25km beyond the defensive walls of the Roman town built in *c* AD 190–220. Attempts have been made to establish the limits of the *territorium* of the city – as distinct from the economic hinterland which served the city – but these have been largely inconclusive (for example Merrifield 1983, 127–34.). It is likely that the eastern boundary of the *territorium* lay at the River Lea, thus placing the study area within the area directly controlled by the city (see Fig 2).

The most intensively studied aspect of the east London hinterland in recent years has been the eastern Roman cemetery (Barber et al 1990; Barber and Bowsher 2000). The full extent of the cemetery is not known: its western edge was more or less coincident with the later city wall and its northern limit seems to have lain close to the line of the road between Aldgate and Old Ford. The greatest uncertainty concerns the southern and eastern limits of the cemetery, largely because the recent excavations did not extend far enough in these directions to uncover evidence of the cemetery boundaries. The area of the cemetery was divided into plots and an east–west aligned road formed the axis upon which the plots were laid out. Extraction of sand and gravel seems to have taken place before the first burials were interred. The road was constructed *c* AD 70–80 and continued in use until the late 3rd century; the first burials can be dated to the late 1st or early 2nd century. Burials continued to take place until the very end of the Roman period. The Shadwell sites lay some 500m east of the easternmost site within the east London cemetery study area. A number of antiquarian observations (Hall 1996) recorded burials to the north and east of the Shadwell sites along the line of The

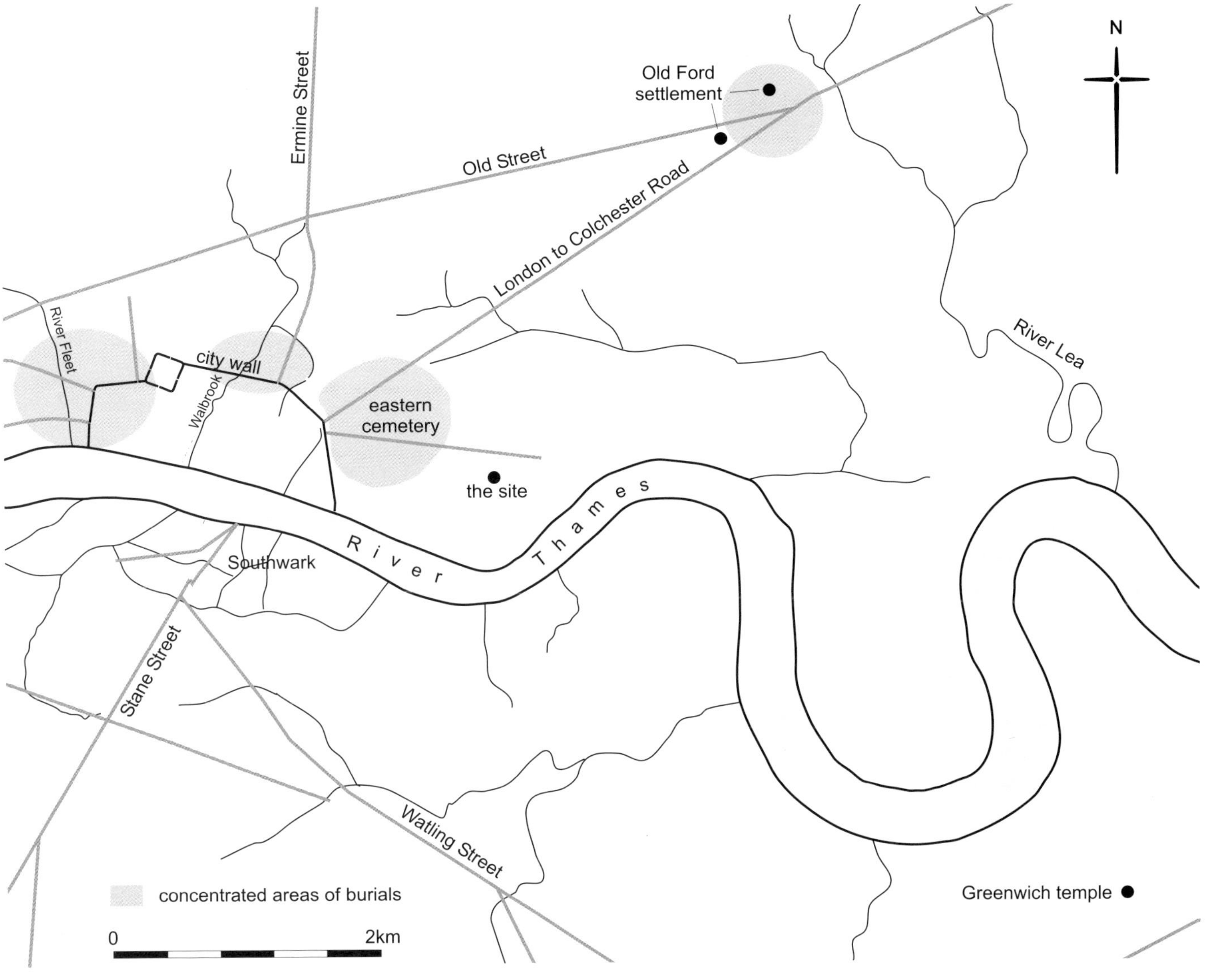

Fig 2 *Eastern hinterland of Roman London (scale 1:50,000)*

Highway; the date, location and validity of these observations must, however, be the subject of some doubt.

A settlement at Ratcliff, on the River Thames to the east of Shadwell, has been suggested, although there is almost no archaeological evidence yet for such a settlement. Merrifield has speculated that the modern line of The Highway follows the course of a Roman road running eastwards from Londinium to the Ratcliff 'settlement' along the edge of the gravel escarpment (Merrifield 1983, 133). Archaeological evidence to support the existence of such a road might be sought in recent work in the eastern cemetery: here the east–west axial road through the cemetery may have formed an eastward extension of the city road grid to serve the cemetery, or alternatively may have been intended to link the city with a hinterland settlement (Barber and Bowsher 2000, 51–2, figs 3, 9). The road seems to have predated the first burials in the cemetery and certainly extended beyond the eastern limit of the cemetery study area, perhaps suggesting that purpose of the road was not solely connected with the cemetery. Its ultimate destination might perhaps be sought in the area to the east of the cemetery. A simple eastward extrapolation of the road's known alignment would meet the River Thames near Ratcliff; it would not, however, follow the escarpment edge route suggested by Merrifield and would pass *c* 100m north of the Shadwell sites.

Roman remains noted at Old Ford, Bow, clearly indicate the presence of a roadside settlement (Sheldon 1972; McIsaac et al 1979). Here, the development of the Aldgate to Colchester road was demonstrated along with the presence of domestic and industrial structures, and field ditches. All of the structures relating to the settlement were dated to the 4th century, but the discovery in the vicinity of much earlier burials and 2nd- to 3rd-century field ditches suggests a greater lifespan for the settlement, excavated evidence for which may be lacking owing to the small-scale nature of the excavations undertaken.

It has been suggested (Sheldon 1972, 128), based on the large quantity of butchered cattle bones from the excavations, that the Old Ford settlement may have played a role in provisioning Londinium. A brick-lined pit noted in the Lefevre Road excavations at Old Ford may have formed part of a tile kiln, indicating the industrial function which may also have been served by some of Londinium's hinterland settlements (Sheldon 1972, 52).

Table 1 Summary of Shadwell chronology

Date	Period		Phase	
Natural	1	geology and topography	1	natural drift geology
1st to early 2nd century AD	2	quarrying and cremation burials	2	brickearth quarrying
			3	cremation burials
3rd century AD	3	landscape reorganisation	4	post-built structure
			5	widespread pitting
			6	boundary ditches and timber buildng
			7	disuse of timber building and replacement ditches
Mid 4th century AD	4	industrial activity	8	timber-lined tanks, drains and metalling
Late 4th century AD	5	inhumation burials and abandonment of the site	9	demolition deposit and inhumation burials
			10	disuse, soil accumulation

Table 2 Roman pottery fabric codes

Code	Description	Ware group
AHFA	Alice Holt/Farnham ware	reduced ware
AHSU	Alice Holt/Surrey ware	reduced ware
AMPH	miscellaneous amphora fabric type	amphorae
AMPH1-7	amphorae	amphorae
BAET	Baetican Dressel 20 amphora fabric	amphorae
BB1	black-burnished type 1 ware	black-burnished type ware
BB2	black-burnished type 2 ware	black-burnished type ware
BBS	black-burnished style ware	black-burnished type ware
BIV	late Roman Biv amphora fabric	amphorae
CALC	late Roman shell-gritted ware (formerly 'calcite-tempered')	tempered ware
CC	miscellaneous colour-coated wares	miscellaneous ware
CGBL	Central Gaulish/Lezoux black colour-coated ware	imported fine ware
COAR	miscellaneous coarse ware	tempered ware
EPON	céramique à l'éponge	imported fine ware
FINE	miscellaneous fine ware	fine reduced ware
GAUL1	Pélichet 47/Dressel 30 amphora fabric	amphorae
HWC	Highgate 'C' sand-tempered ware	reduced ware
KOLN	Cologne colour-coated ware	imported fine ware
LOXI	local oxidised ware	oxidised ware
MAYEN	Mayen ware	oxidised ware
MICA	miscellaneous mica-dusted ware	Romano-British fine ware
MOSL	Moselkeramik	imported fine ware
NAFR	North African amphora fabric, not distinguished	amphorae
NAFR1	North African lime-rich amphora fabric	amphorae
NGGW	North Gaulish grey ware	reduced ware
NGWH	North Gaulish white ware	oxidised ware
NKWS	North Kent red- and white-slipped ware	oxidised ware
NVCC	Nene Valley colour-coated ware	Romano-British fine ware
OXID	miscellaneous oxidised ware	oxidised ware
OXPA	Oxfordshire parchment ware	oxidised ware
OXRC	Oxfordshire red/brown colour-coated ware	Romano-British fine ware
OXWW	Oxfordshire white ware	oxidised ware
PORD	Portchester 'D' ware	oxidised ware
RHWW	Rhineland white ware (other than Soller)	oxidised ware
RWS	miscellaneous red- and white-slipped ware	oxidised ware
SAM	samian ware	samian ware
SAMCG	Central Gaulish samian ware	samian ware
SAMEG	East Gaulish samian ware	samian ware
SAMLG	La Graufesenque samian ware	samian ware
SAND	miscellaneous sand-tempered ware	reduced ware
SPEC	Speicher ware	oxidised ware
VCWS	Verulamium region coarse white-slipped ware	oxidised ware
VRW	Verulamium region white ware	oxidised ware

1.3 Organisation of this report

Following the Introduction, the stratigraphic sequence is discussed in Chapter 2, incorporating discussion of the finds, especially key pottery and the animal bone assemblages. The stratigraphic sequence is described in terms of land use, with Buildings, Open Areas, Roads and Structures (sometimes here abbreviated to B, OA, R and S). Each of these elements is fitted into a chronology, based mainly upon ceramic and coin dating together with stratigraphic relationships, to form a period and phase framework. Phases form the basic chronological divisions. They have been grouped into five periods which are particular to the Shadwell sites and which are defined by basic, broad, site functions and their changes (Table 1). The character of the Roman sequence is discussed in Chapter 3 with particular emphasis on the function of the masonry 'tower', with more general conclusions made in Chapter 4. The methodologies used for, and a catalogue of, the principal results from the finds and animal bone assemblages are given in Chapter 5. Full expansions of the pottery codes used are in Davies et al (1994) for the early period and Symonds and Tomber (1991) for the later period (Tables 2–4).

Table 3 Roman pottery form codes

Code	Description
Flagon	
1	unidentified flagon
1B7–9	cup-mouthed ring-necked flagon
1D	disc-mouthed flagon
1H	flagon with continuous body
1L	disc-necked flagon
Jar	
2	unidentified jar
2/3	jar or beaker; enclosed vessel
2A	bead-rimmed jar
2A17	black-burnished type bead-rimmed jar
2C	necked jar with carinated shoulder; 'figure 7' rim
2D	round-bodied necked jar with 'figure 7' rim
2E	round-bodied necked jar with burnished shoulder
2F	black-burnished type everted-rimmed jar
2F13	black-burnished type cavetto-rimmed jar
2FX	late AHFA version of 2F jar
2G	necked jar; usually with cordon at shoulder
2H	large neckless jar with near-horizontal rim
2J	neckless 'unguent' jar
2R	narrow-necked jar/flask
2T	otherwise indistinguishable necked jar
2W	hook-rimmed jar
Beaker	
3	unidentified beaker
3Déch 67	Déchelette form 67 beaker
3Déch 68	Déchelette form 68 beaker
3E	beaker with short everted rim
3F	'poppyhead' beaker
3J	bag-shaped beaker
3K	necked globular beaker
3L	pentice beaker
Bowl	
4	unidentified bowl
4A	reed-rimmed bowl
4/5	bowl/dish
4C306	Camulodunum type 306 bowl with 'D-shaped' rim
4CU21	Curle form 21 bowl
4DR29	Dragendorff form 29 bowl
4DR30	Dragendorff form 30 bowl
4DR31/37R	Dragendorff form 31/37R bowl
4DR37	Dragendorff form 37 bowl
4DR38	Dragendorff form 38 bowl
4G	flat-rimmed bowl with vertical wall
4G226	bowl with incipient flange (Gillam form 226)
4H	round-rimmed black-burnished type bowl
4Lud Sa	Ludowici form Sa bowl
4Lud Sb	Ludowici form Sb bowl
4Lud SMbc	Ludowici form SMb/SMc bowl
4M	black-burnished type flanged bowl
4Q	tripod bowl
4WA81	Walters form 81 bowl
Plate/dish	
5	unidentified plate
5CU15	Curle form 15 dish
5DR15/17	Dragendorff form 15/17 dish
5DR18	Dragendorff form 18 dish
5DR18R	Dragendorff form 18R dish
5DR18/31	Dragendorff form 18/31 dish
Plate/dish (cont)	
5DR31	Dragendorff form 31 dish
5DR31R	Dragendorff form 31R dish
5DR31/33	Dragendorff form 31/33 dish
5DR32	Dragendorff form 32 dish
5DR36	Dragendorff form 36 dish
5J	dish with simple rim
5Lud Tg	Ludowici form Tg dish
5Lud TgR	Ludowici form TgR dish
5Lud Tk	Ludowici form Tk dish
5WA79	Walters form 79
5WA79R	Walters form 79R dish
Cup	
6DR27	Dragendorff form 27 cup
6DR33	Dragendorff form 33 cup
6DR35	Dragendorff form 35 cup
6Knorr 78	Knorr form 78 cup
Mortarium	
7	unidentified mortarium
7DR43	Dragendorff form 43 mortarium
7DR45	Dragendorff form 45 mortarium
7HAM	hammerhead mortarium
7HOF	hook-flanged mortarium
7LWAL	late wall-sided mortarium
7M17	Young type M17 mortarium
7M22	Young type M22 mortarium
Amphora	
8	miscellaneous amphorae
8DR2–4	Dressel form 2–4 amphorae
8DR20	Dressel form 20 amphora
8G	Pélichet 47/Dressel form 30/Gauloise-type amphora
Box/lid	
9A	lid
9G	castor box
9GL	castor box lid

Table 4 Roman pottery decoration codes

Code	Description
ARCX	arcs on later black-burnished ware forms
BAD	barbotine decoration
BDD	barbotine dot decoration
BFD	barbotine figure decoration
BUD	burnished decoration
CL	curvilinear decoration
OL	obtuse lattice decoration
RND	round indentations
ROD	rouletted decoration
SCD	barbotine scale decoration
SCR	barbotine scroll decoration
SPT	spout
STD	stamped decoration
UND	unidentified indentations
WBAD	white barbotine decoration

1.4 Textual and graphical conventions used in this report

The basic unit of cross-reference throughout the archive that supports this report is the context number. This is a unique number given to each archaeological event on site (such as a layer, wall, pit cut or road surface). Each context number is prefixed by the sitecode, thus: LD76 [100], and each accessioned find number, thus: LD74 <210>. As the finds are drawn from both sites, LD74 and LD76, into a single corpus of material, in this report they do not bear the site code prefix, but instead the catalogue is divided into categories of finds which have been numbered internally and an appropriate letter prefix used thus:

<S10> accessioned finds (excluding glass)
<G10> glass object
<P10> illustrated non-samian pottery sherd
<SAM10> decorated samian ware

Graphical conventions are shown in Fig 3.

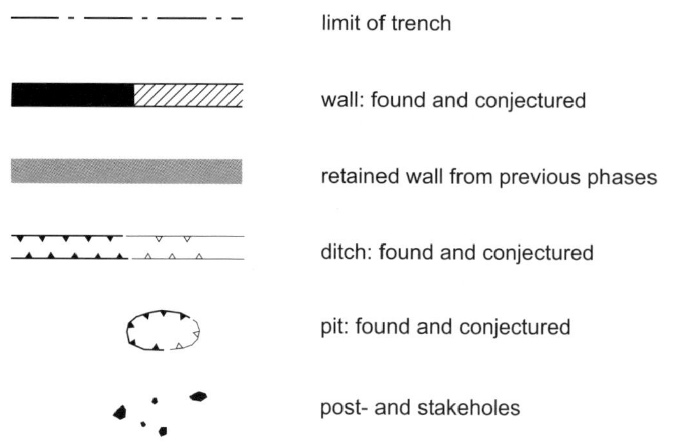

Fig 3 Graphical conventions used in this report

2

The archaeological sequence

2.1 Period 1: geology and topography

Phase 1: natural drift geology

The Shadwell sites lay at the edge of the Thames River Terrace close to the point where the post-glacial course of the river has left a marked escarpment. The sands and gravels which constitute the terrace are generally capped by deposits of windblown silts (Langley Silts or brickearth). Immediately north of the sites, the modern ground level along The Highway lies at between 9.00m OD and 9.50m OD but drops away sharply towards the south to a minimum of 5.20m OD. The sites are located *c* 500m from the modern course of the Thames.

Natural deposits and topography were poorly recorded on both sites, though it appears that they lay on brickearth, and section information suggests that the maximum height of natural was *c* 4.50m OD (OA1). The current topography of the area exhibits a marked slope down to the south from an east–west aligned escarpment in the vicinity of the site. Incidental references in the archives for both sites suggest that the area had been levelled up by the deposition of imported material in the 19th century. Consequently, the escarpment was probably much more marked in the Roman period. Section evidence from LD74 indicates that the escarpment slope started within 5.0m of the southern edge of that site, although there is no corresponding evidence from LD76. Observations during construction work at 172–176 The Highway and 9 Wapping Lane (HIH95), immediately west of LD74, indicate that the natural ground surface was fairly level towards the west, brickearth being observed at a general height of *c* 4.60m OD. The sites seem to have been located on the flat top of a brickearth bluff, the slope of which fell sharply away to the south close to the limits of excavation.

2.2 Period 2: 1st- to early 2nd-century quarrying and cremation burials

Phase 2: brickearth quarrying

The first activity noted at the Shadwell sites was brickearth quarrying, which took place from the Flavian period onwards and was concentrated in the eastern part of LD76 (phase 2, Fig 4). This was accompanied by small-scale levelling or similar activity which resulted in the redeposition of brickearth, sand and gravel across the whole site (OA2 and OA3). The pottery from the period 2 features ranges in date from the 1st to 4th centuries. The earliest dated samian from phase 2 includes a South Gaulish (SAMLG) Dragendorff (Drag) 29 (<SAM1>, Fig 17) dated to *c* AD 65–85. Finds from the redeposited material within the quarry pit are dated to AD 70–90 by a SAMLG Drag 37 bowl, (<SAM3>, Fig 17) and two Drag 18 dishes; other

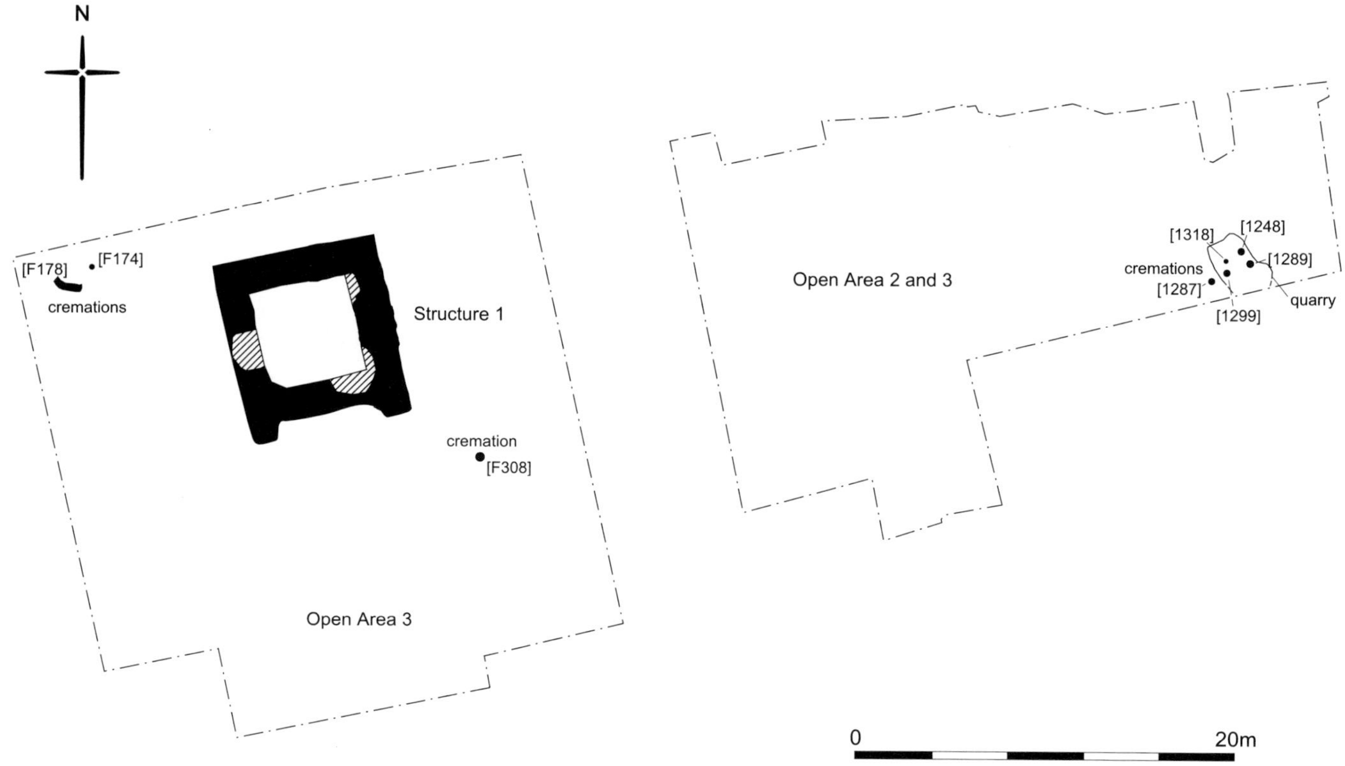

Fig 4 Open Areas 2 and 3, quarrying and cremation burials, and Structure 1, the 'tower', in period 2, phases 2 and 3 (scale 1:400)

material dating from the 2nd to 4th centuries was also recovered from these deposits indicating that the material accumulated over a long period or, more probably, that it was subject to disturbance as a result of later activity. The lack of evidence datable to this period from LD74 is more likely a reflection of the nature of the surviving records from this site than a genuine absence of activity at this date. Very few objects of Roman date were found in the redeposited brickearth and gravels: these included glassware <G73> and a bone pin (not catalogued) but, with the exception of two intrusive coins of AD 270–82 and AD 253–73, all are fragmentary.

Phase 3: cremation burials

The brickearth quarrying was followed by the deposition of up to nine cremation burials (phase 3, Fig 4) found in two distinct clusters. In the south-east corner of LD76 were five cremation burials, of which four had been inserted into the backfill of the earlier quarry, with a fifth immediately adjacent to the quarry pit on its western side. A second cluster of three cremation burials was located in the north-west corner of LD74, with a single outlier towards the centre of the site.

The cremations (with the possible exception of the outlier from LD74) were all contained within ceramic vessels (Fig 5). The cremations from LD74 were described by the excavator as being contained in vessels of late 2nd-century date, although no specific identifications were made (the vessels were not available at the time of this study). The five cremation burials from LD76 were all contained in vessels which can be dated to the first half of the 2nd century, although there was one abraded sherd of Nene Valley colour-coated ware (NVCC) from the infill of cremation LD76 [1299], dated post-AD 150.

Cremation burial <P1>–<P2>, LD76 [1299]

The cremation vessel is a large Verulamium region white ware necked jar (VRW 2G) (<P1>, Fig 5). This vessel is complete, although now in eleven sherds. The rim is squared off with an internal lid-seating groove. The internal rim diameter is 190mm. It also has a groove at the junction of the neck to the body. This type of jar is generally dated to the late 1st and 2nd centuries, with later examples tending to have narrower bodies and none of the cordons or grooves which are present on the earlier examples (Marsh and Tyers 1979, 562, fig 237 nos II.G.1–3). This vessel has none of these later characteristics, suggesting it is probably earlier (late 1st to early 2nd century) rather than later in date. The other nearly-complete vessel from this context is a reduced sand-tempered ware lid (SAND 9A) (<P2>, Fig 5) with a diameter of 200mm. Although not found *in situ*, this was probably the lid of the cremation vessel.

Cremation burial <P3>–<P4>, LD76 [1318]

The cremation vessel is an Alice Holt Surrey ware necked jar with carinated shoulder (AHSU 2C2) (<P3>, Fig 5) dated to AD 50–150. This jar has the distinctive 'figure 7' rim of the

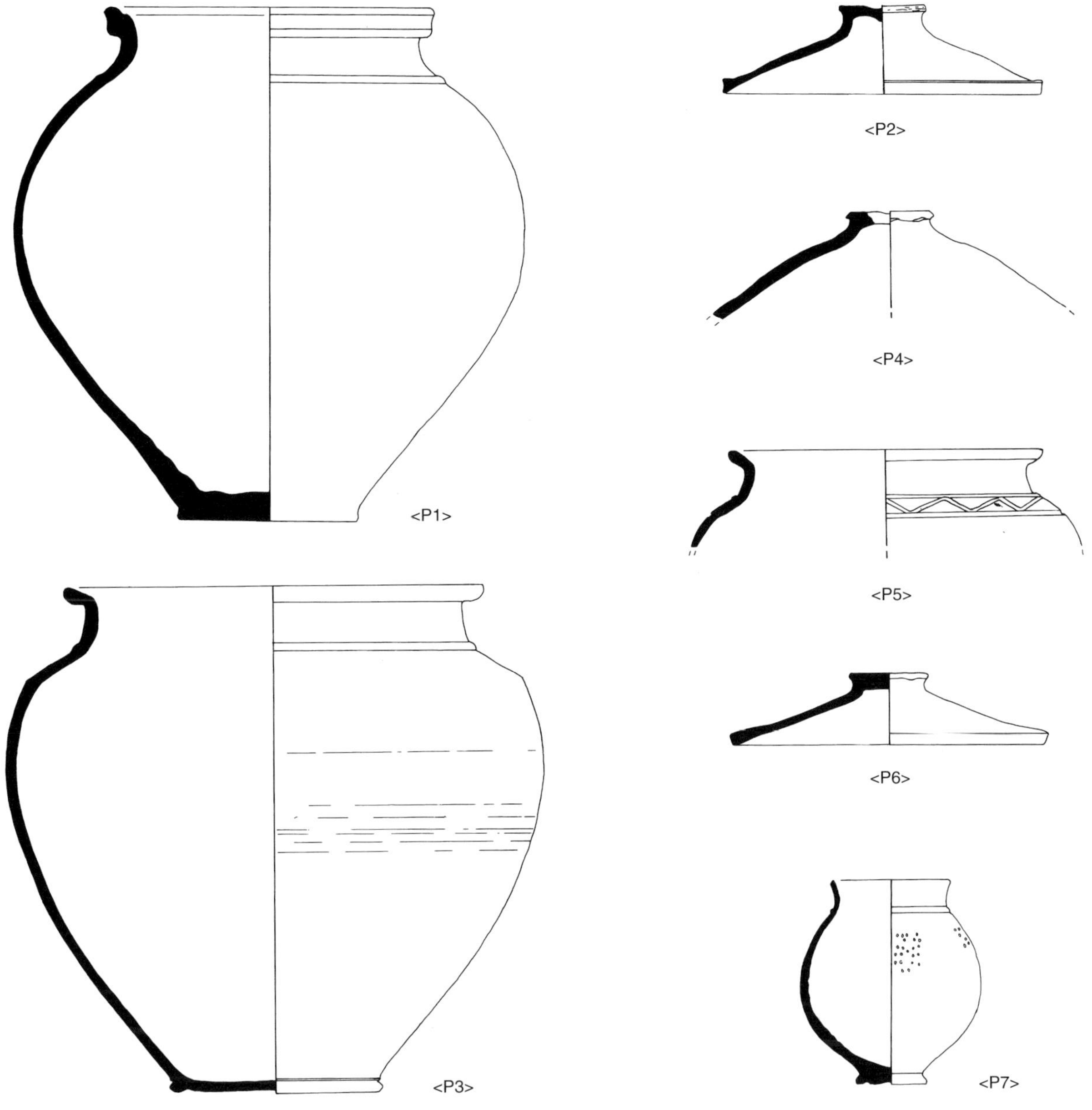

Fig 5 Ceramic cremation vessels and lids <P1>–<P7> (scale 1:4)

subtype 2C2 (Marsh and Tyers 1979, 559, fig 235 no. IIC2) and there is evidence on the lower part of the body of knife trimming. The surfaces are abraded, possibly due to soil conditions, a feature also of many of the burial and cremation vessels from the cemetery at Great Dover Street in Southwark (Seeley 2000, 55). The jar, which was found crushed *in situ*, is incomplete with a portion of the rim missing. The internal diameter of the vessel is *c* 220mm.

Within the cremation vessel were two large sherds of a local oxidised ware lid (LOXI 9A) (<P4>, Fig 5) dated to AD 90–160. As the jar was found smashed *in situ*, it is not improbable that if there was a lid on top, this may also have been broken, and sherds may have fallen into the jar when it was damaged. The edges of the two sherds are softened and abraded, consistent with being broken in antiquity (as are most of the sherds of the jar). The two other sherds from within the cremation are too small and abraded to influence the date.

Cremation burial LD76 [1248]

The vessel from this cremation was found broken *in situ* and, apart from one rim sherd, only the base and lower part of the body survive. It is a wheel-thrown Alice Holt Surrey ware (AHSU) necked jar (2T) (vessel not illustrated). From the surviving rim sherd it is not possible to define whether the vessel is a necked jar with a sharply carinated shoulder (2C) or a necked round-shouldered jar (2D) as both types can have the same 'figure 7' rim and a cordon at the junction of the neck and body. The surfaces are damaged possibly by soil conditions and the edges of some of the sherds are softened, suggesting that the vessel was broken in antiquity. Rather than the usual grey, the surfaces of some sherds are slightly orange in colour especially on the neck; this is possibly the result of burning and may suggest that the vessel is reused.

Cremation burial LD76 [1289]

According to the original site records this cremation was found in a broken bowl, but the vessel is missing.

Cremation burial <P5>–<P7>, LD76 [1287]

Three vessels are associated with this cremation burial (illustrated on front cover). There is a reduced sand-tempered ware jar (<P5>, Fig 5); its fabric is so friable that the vessel albeit complete is now in *c* 120 sherds. This vessel has not been reconstructed and only the rim is illustrated here. The fabric of this jar is problematic: although the sorting and size of the quartz is similar to that of Alice Holt Surrey ware, it is unusually iron-rich and friable for this ware. The vessel is a necked round-shouldered jar with a 'figure 7' rim (2D). Additionally there is burnished decoration on the shoulder. A fine reduced-ware lid (FINE 9A) (<P6>, Fig 5) was found covering the jar. This lid is complete, although now in four fragments. The diameter of the lid and the external diameter of the jar are both 185mm.

The third vessel associated with this cremation is a Highgate 'C' ware (HWC) 'poppyhead' beaker with barbotine dot decoration (3F4 BDD; <P7>, Fig 5). The vessel is the sub-type 3F4 which is dated to the first half of the 2nd century (Marsh and Tyers 1979, 570, fig 239, no. III.F.4). All three of the vessels have damaged surfaces; this is especially evident on the beaker where the glossy surface typical of these vessels in HWC has been completely removed and the raised barbotine dots are either totally lost or only visible as 'shadows' on the surface.

Burial rites

Three of the cremation burial vessels are accompanied by lids and, although not all of the lids were found *in situ* on top of the jars, their diameters are very similar to those of the corresponding vessels. A similar practice is observed in the cremation burials dated to the 2nd century in Roman London's eastern cemetery (Barber and Bowsher 2000, 432–5, table 9). Additionally the absence of samian among the burial vessels at Shadwell echoes the trend seen in the much larger cemetery, where no samian forms were used in burials or cremations (Symonds 2000, 123–4). Another feature of the Shadwell vessels is the poor condition of the surfaces which is similar to those from the cemetery at Great Dover Street and is possibly a result of soil conditions (Seeley 2000, 55).

The only non-ceramic objects associated with these burials were an iron nail and four fragments of vessel glass (not catalogued) found with burial LD76 [1287]. None of the human remains from any of the cremation burials was available at the time of writing. Correspondence in the Shadwell site archives suggests that a study of the remains from LD76 had previously been undertaken but there is no report of the results.

Structure 1: masonry 'tower'

Some consideration of what may be thought to be the principal feature of the study area, the masonry 'tower', has been undertaken at this point in the narrative largely because the available records do not allow the structure to be dated either absolutely or in relation to any of the other features. All the features, except one, that postdate the disuse of the mid 4th-century industrial phase, also postdate the destruction of the 'tower'. Structure 1 may, therefore, be contemporary with any or all of the phases of periods 2 and 3 (Figs 4, 7–10).

The available records do not provide a full description of the structure, though the following deductions may be made. It was approximately 9.0m square externally and a little over 5.0m square internally (Fig 6). The walls were *c* 1.90m thick and were composed of mortared flint and chalk (possibly also ragstone). Two slight buttresses projected from the south-east and south-west corners. The foundations were approximately 0.45m deep. The structure had been extensively robbed: only the east wall and a part of the north wall survived and those remained to a height of no more than 300mm above contemporary ground level. This was sufficient, however, to show that the lowest two courses of masonry were faced externally with knapped flint laid in 'herringbone' style with at least one tile course above; the tile course did not penetrate the full thickness of the wall. The wall core above ground was composed of the same material as the foundation. Almost all of the interior of the structure had been truncated by later features; in the north-east corner, however, some elements of the interior construction survived. A thin layer of gravel marked the construction horizon and was level with the contemporary external ground surface. Above this lay a deposit of clay and sand which came to just below the level of the surviving masonry (the feature list from LD74 notes that this deposit contained a fragment of Castor ware hunt cup; see below) and was in turn capped by a further thin layer of sand. There was no evidence from the surviving masonry elements of any entrance or other openings. If these existed they must have lain in the western or southern sides. A large crack in the eastern wall indicates that the south-eastern buttress had shifted away from the rest of the structure.

The original excavator identified the structure as a signal tower, but this should now be considered to be highly speculative. Its form and construction do not immediately suggest a function. The potentially associated features vary from quarry pits and cremation burials to possible tanning pits. Too few finds were directly associated with the structure to suggest any function for it. Only one item from both sites' finds assemblages was of definitely military type (<S26>), fewer than usually found on civilian sites in the London area. The samian assemblage may, however, hint at some military presence in the vicinity of the site. The function of this structure is considered at greater length in Chapters 3 and 4.

Its date is equally difficult to define. The presence in its construction deposits of a sherd from a Castor ware hunt cup would certainly suggest a construction date after AD 150;

Fig 6 *View of the excavation at LD74 from the north: (centre) the masonry 'tower' (S1); (top) the east–west boundary ditches (S4, S8, S9); (left) drain (S10) (2.0m scale)*

however, this sherd is no longer available for study and its identification must be seen as highly speculative. The backfill in the robbed foundations of the structure contained a coin of AD 355–65, clearly indicating that it had gone out of use by this date. The presence of masonry rubble in the fills of the phase 7 gullies may indicate that the structure had gone out of use and was being dismantled by the 340s. On the other hand, the fact that the mid 4th-century industrial structures did not impinge on the building may indicate that it was still substantially intact in the 350s or later. The demolition material from the disuse of these industrial features, which abutted the surviving east wall of the structure, also contained coins datable to as late as AD 365, indicating final destruction in or after the 360s.

2.3 Period 3: 3rd-century landscape reorganisation

Phase 4: post-built structure and gully

The next period of activity was characterised by the absence of burials and the appearance of post-built structures on both LD76 and LD74 (phase 4, Fig 7). It is difficult to define the structures represented by these features or indeed to determine how many structures were present. What seems clear is that, in the absence of associated surfaces, no structural elements were within a building. The postholes on LD74 formed a clear

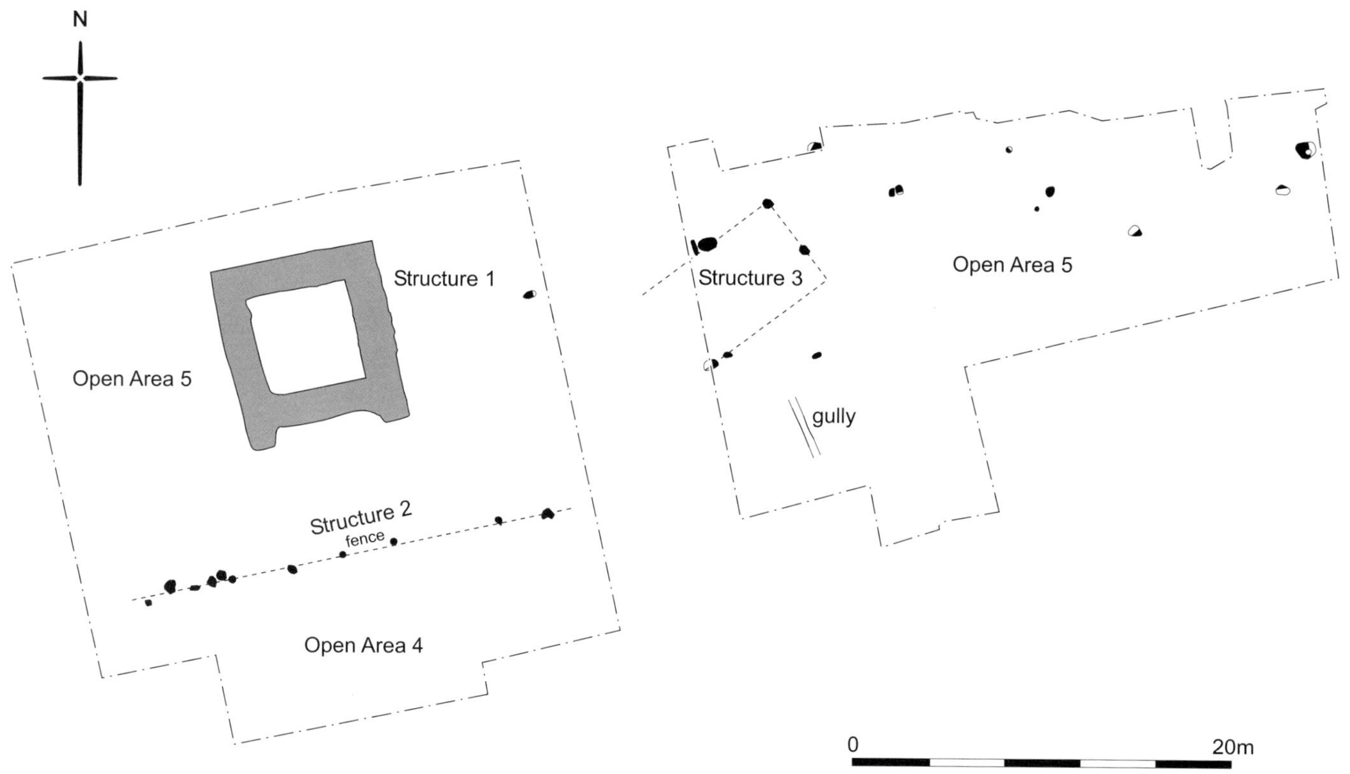

Fig 7 3rd-century landscape reorganisation in period 3, phase 4 (scale 1:400)

east–west alignment, which almost exactly mirrored that of a later gully, and are probably to be interpreted as a boundary fence (S2), perpetuated by later ditches and gullies and dividing Open Area 4 to the south from Open Area 5 to the north. The postholes on LD76 were much less clearly ordered, although it is possible tentatively to reconstruct alignments. It is probable that the high degree of later truncation has obscured any original patterning of these features and likely that they too once formed part of a boundary fence or fences (S3) in OA5.

A short section of north–south aligned gully in the south-west corner of LD76 has also been assigned to this phase, largely on the basis that it must predate the later ditch. The fills of the gully suggest drainage although the high degree of truncation to which it was subject has removed any related features which might have confirmed this interpretation. A coin of AD 270–3 was found in this gully.

Little datable material was recovered from the features in this phase, and what little there was could usually only be attributed generally to the Roman period. There is a small assemblage of pottery from the post-built structures. The pottery within these features dates from the mid to later 3rd century, with only one sherd of Oxfordshire red/brown colour-coated ware (OXRC) dating the group to post-AD 270, and its identification is uncertain. Otherwise the group is dated by NVCC beakers and by black-burnished 1 (BB1) ware flanged (4M) and incipient-flanged (4G226) bowls. No samian was found in this assemblage. A mid to late 3rd-century date is also supported by a coin dated AD 270–3. This seems to indicate a continuum of activity with the pit and ditch digging which followed.

Phase 5: widespread pitting

The next phase of activity (phase 5) was characterised by widespread pitting on LD76 in Open Area 5 (Fig 8). The nature of the record precluded the identification of a similar phase on site LD74, although it should be noted that a number of pits recorded on that site remain to be assigned and might possibly belong to this phase. The pits noted on LD76 were generally shallow and irregular in form and of indeterminate function. Finds from the features were scarce and undiagnostic. The pits produced fragments of two glass drinking vessels, a hemispherical cup <G34> and a greenish-colourless beaker <G64>, both of which date from the 3rd or 4th century (Fig 24). The only other identifiable objects were coins, most of late 3rd-century date.

The animal bone from eight of the pits, a combined total of 74 fragments (2.22kg), is considered here as one assemblage (see OA5, Table 15). The majority of the faunal remains were recovered from just two of these features with 43 and 26 fragments respectively. As can be seen in Table 15, the great majority of this group is composed of cattle and cattle-sized fragments. Within the cattle assemblage, there is a notably high representation of skull (especially mandible) and foot parts, that is, metapodials and phalanges (see OA5, Table 16). It is conceivable that a large proportion of this assemblage was derived from butchery, these parts being set aside during the dressing of the carcass. Alternatively, the concentration of such parts may indicate industrial waste. Amongst the metapodials was one fragment which clearly belonged to a very young individual, probably neonate. The presence of this age group is a strong indicator of local breeding, the young calf representing an infant mortality.

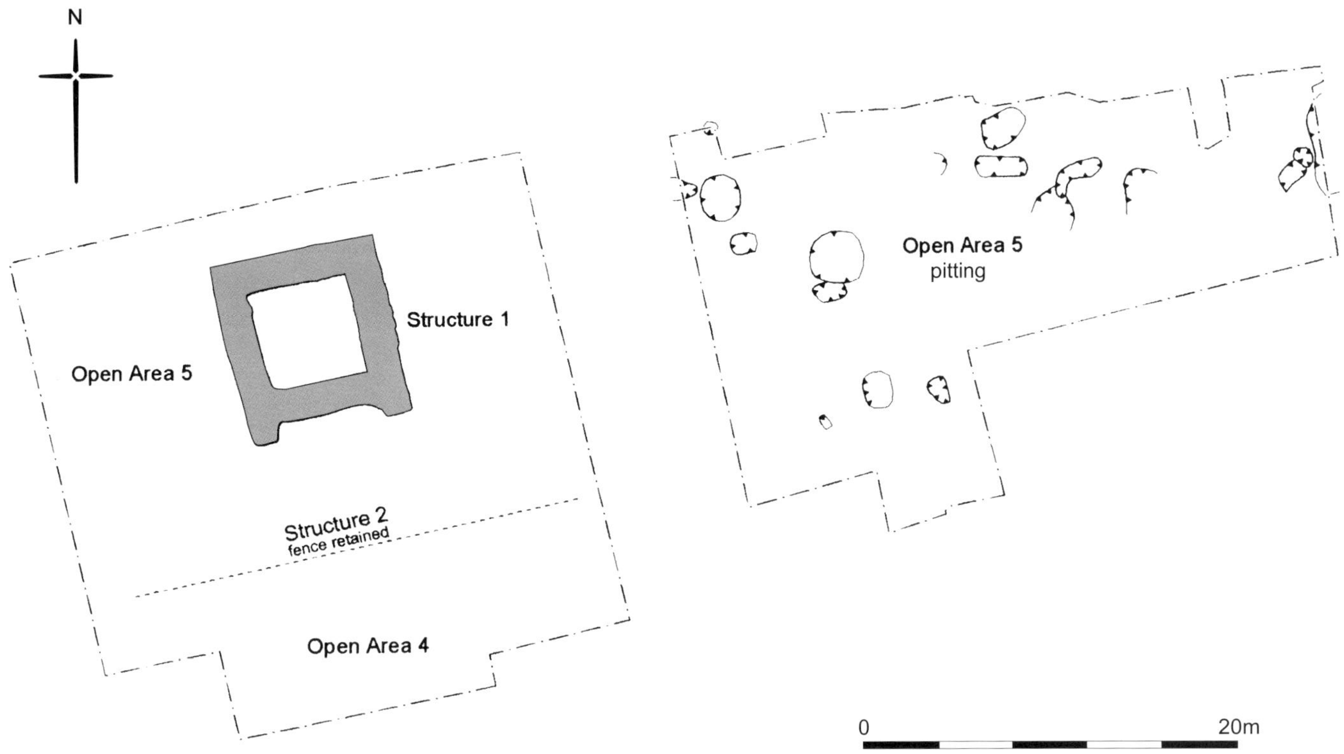

Fig 8 *3rd-century pitting, period 3, phase 5 (scale 1:400)*

Each of the remaining species recovered from these pitfills is very poorly represented. Most, with the possible exception of dog, can be interpreted as food waste. One of the small mammal bones, a cervical vertebra, had been chopped, both transversely and sagitally. The method of butchery would seem to suggest that this animal was used for its meat. Unfortunately the species could not positively be identified, the question remaining whether it represents a typical food animal such as hare, or a rather unusual food item, such as dog or cat.

Pottery was recovered from numerous pits in Open Area 5 (a total of 7.66 EVEs, estimated vessel equivalents, or 7828g; Tables 5–6). Overall the pottery from these pits is dated to the mid–later 3rd century. This date is supported by coins dating AD 268–70 in LD76 [351], AD 270–85 in LD76 [189] and AD 270–80 in LD76 [1250]. There are no decorated samian forms from the deposits in this open area. The plain samian forms are mostly of East Gaulish manufacture and generally dated from the later 2nd to the mid 3rd century.

The two reduced fabrics, black-burnished 1 (BB1) and Alice Holt Farnham ware (AHFA), are present in almost equal quantities. Nene Valley colour-coated ware (NVCC) is the predominant fine ware (excluding samian) from this phase, although Oxfordshire red/brown colour-coated ware (OXRC) is present, confirming its generally accepted first appearance in London as *c* AD 270. Beakers are the single most common form in NVCC, with scale and white barbotine scroll decoration occurring frequently. The scale decoration occurs on funnel-necked folded beakers, a type dated from the second quarter of the 3rd century (Perrin 1999, 94). White barbotine, as a type of decoration on NVCC beakers, is more common after the mid 3rd century (ibid, 98). There is also an NVCC pentice beaker (3L), a form that is not well dated in this fabric and thought possibly to be 4th century in date (Howe et al 1980, 22; Perrin 1999, 97). However, recent work on a large well group from 107 Borough High Street, Southwark (107BHS81), which contained at least two NVCC pentice beakers (with pottery dating to *c* AD 250–70 and two coins of Tetricus dating to the 270s–280s), supports a late 3rd-century date for their first appearance in London (Seeley in prep). One pit contains an unusual form, a jar with a flanged rim, in BB1. This form occurs at Exeter (Holbrook and Bidwell 1991, 106, fig 29 no. 28.1) where it is dated from the mid to late 3rd century onwards. The dating evidence for this pit includes an overall pottery date of *c* AD 250–400 and a coin dated to AD 268–70.

The high percentage of Highgate 'C' sand-tempered wares in Open Area 5 is due to the presence in one pit LD76 [1296] of a nearly complete, albeit broken, beaker with short everted rim (3E) The high amount of Verulamium region coarse white-slipped wares is due to the presence of a further complete single vessel, in another pit LD76 [1073]. This vessel, a flagon with a continuous body (VCWS 1H), is also smashed and is accompanied by a nearly complete small oxidised ware jar (OXID 2). The ceramic assemblages from both these pits are notably earlier in date than those from other pits in this phase. They are dated AD 70–120 (LD76 [1073]) and, by the presence of NVCC, AD 150–200 (LD76 [1296]), although as the assemblages are small these dates should be treated with some caution. The condition of these vessels and their early date (compared with the rest of the pottery from the pits in this open area) suggests that they may be from disturbed burials or cremations belonging to the previous phase of use (period 2, phase 3).

Table 5 Pottery fabric quantities from pits in Open Area 5

Ware group	Fabric code	Rows	% rows	EVEs	% EVEs	Weight (g)	% weight
Amphorae	AMPH	3	2.3	0	–	339	4.3
	AMPH1	4	3.1	0	–	20	0.3
	AMPH2	1	0.8	0	–	5	0.1
	AMPH3	1	0.8	0	–	155	2.0
	AMPH4	1	0.8	0	–	256	3.3
	BAET	1	0.8	0	–	70	0.9
	BIV	1	0.8	0	–	1	<0.1
	GAUL1	4	3.1	0	–	2001	25.6
Samian ware	SAMCG	4	3.1	0.3	3.9	63	0.8
	SAMEG	7	5.5	0.86	11.2	148	1.9
	SAMLG	1	0.8	0	–	23	0.3
Imported fine ware	MOSL	3	2.3	0	–	21	0.3
Romano-British fine ware	NVCC	20	15.6	0.3	3.9	245	3.1
	OXRC	2	1.6	0.05	0.7	64	0.8
Black-burnished type ware	BB1	9	7.0	0.61	8.0	438	5.6
	BB2	2	1.6	0.2	2.6	107	1.4
	BBS	9	7.0	1.04	13.6	440	5.6
Reduced ware	AHFA	9	7.0	0.7	9.1	380	4.9
	HWC	1	0.8	0.9	11.7	108	1.4
	SAND	22	17.2	0.3	3.9	942	12.0
Oxidised ware	MAYEN	1	0.8	0	–	22	0.3
	NKWS	1	0.8	0	–	35	0.4
	OXID	12	9.4	1.16	15.1	461	5.9
	OXWW	1	0.8	0	–	15	0.2
	VCWS	1	0.8	1	13.1	843	10.8
	VRW	5	3.9	0.18	2.3	604	7.7
Miscellaneous	CC	2	1.6	0.06	0.8	22	0.3
Totals		**128**	**100.0**	**7.66**	**100.0**	**7828**	**100.0**

See Table 2 for key to fabric codes
Rows: on the Oracle database, each line (row) consists of a unique fabric, form and decoration combination
EVEs: estimated vessel equivalents

Where the pits have stratigraphic relationships with other features it is clear that they post-dated the establishment of the post-built structures of the preceding phase and were truncated by the ditches and associated structures of the subsequent phase. It is possible, therefore, that this phase represents the use of the area organised by divisions established in the previous phase. Although the dating evidence for both is thin it does nonetheless indicate that the two phases probably closely succeeded one another. A distinct alteration in the use of the area is indicated by the cessation of burials followed by land division and pitting. The absence of evidence for associated buildings and occupation deposits calls in question the nature of this new usage. In view of the subsequent establishment of buildings on the site and the quantity of demolition debris recovered from the final Roman phases, any areas of occupation were most likely located nearby but beyond the limits of excavation.

Phase 6: boundary ditches and timber building

Following the establishment of land divisions on the two sites and the use of at least the eastern part of the area for pitting, a further change and intensification in land use can be seen (phase 6, Fig 9). An east–west aligned boundary ditch (S4) replaced the earlier post-built structures and pits, and divided Open Area 6 to the south from Open Area 7 to the north. A further possible boundary ditch (S5) lay at the extreme southern limit of LD76. A rectilinear timber building (B1) lay to the north of the ditches. Associated with this building were internal and external surfaces and at least one further timber structure (S6). Running from north to south across the line of the boundary ditches lay a drain or gully (S7).

Structures 4 and 5: boundary ditches

The boundary ditches (S4 and S5) were quite substantial, up to 2.0m wide and 0.75m deep on LD76. In places, the lower fill

Table 6 Pottery form quantities from pits in Open Area 5

Form	Code	Rows	% rows	EVEs	% EVEs	Weight (g)	% weight
Uncertain	–	23	18.0	0.1	1.3	739	9.4
Flagon	1	3	2.3	0.27	3.5	92	1.2
	1H	1	0.8	1	13.1	843	10.8
Jar	2	19	14.8	1.02	13.3	934	11.9
	2/3	2	1.6	0	–	61	0.8
	2E	1	0.8	0	–	6	0.1
	2FX	2	1.6	0.53	6.9	172	2.2
	2W	1	0.8	0.15	2.0	27	0.3
Beaker	3	20	15.6	0.3	3.9	245	3.1
	3E	1	0.8	0.9	11.7	108	1.4
	3L	1	0.8	0	–	15	0.2
Bowl	4	1	0.8	0.06	0.8	20	0.3
	4/5	7	5.5	0.03	0.4	251	3.2
	4C306	1	0.8	0.1	1.3	23	0.3
	4DR37	2	1.6	0.1	1.3	37	0.5
	4G226	2	1.6	0.26	3.4	52	0.7
	4H	4	3.1	0.42	5.5	182	2.3
	4M	5	3.9	0.46	6.0	190	2.4
Plate/dish	5	1	0.8	0.1	1.3	65	0.8
	5DR18	1	0.8	0	–	23	0.3
	5DR18/31	1	0.8	0.25	3.3	49	0.6
	5DR32	1	0.8	0.24	3.1	11	0.1
	5J	5	3.9	0.62	8.1	289	3.7
	5WA79	1	0.8	0.05	0.7	2	<0.1
Cup	6DR33	2	1.6	0.52	6.8	94	1.2
Mortarium	7	3	2.3	0	–	61	0.8
	7HOF	1	0.8	0.18	2.3	390	5.0
Amphora	8	10	7.8	0	–	520	6.6
	8DR2–4	1	0.8	0	–	256	3.3
	8DR20	1	0.8	0	–	70	0.9
	8G	4	3.1	0	–	2001	25.6
Totals		**128**	**100.0**	**7.66**	**100.0**	**7828**	**100.0**

See Table 3 for key to form codes
Rows: on the Oracle database, each line (row) consists of a unique fabric, form and decoration combination
EVEs: estimated vessel equivalents

of the ditches consisted of sands and gravels which must have eroded from their sides, suggesting that they remained open for a moderate length of time. Given the different profiles demonstrated for Structure 4 on LD76 and LD74, it is possible that a gap or entrance separated the two lengths of ditch, located at the junction of the two sites, a position reinforced by the presence at this point of the north–south drain. Certainly the rounded terminus at the eastern end of the northern ditch on LD76 indicates that there must also have been a gap here. The widespread truncation by later features in the extreme eastern part of that site would have removed any traces of an eastward continuation so the width of any gap is unknown. The position of a further length of ditch (S5), 7.50m south of the principal ditch (S4) on LD76, raises the possibility of a double ditch system with a staggered entrance (similar to that seen in the later gullies; see below, phase 7). A quantity of domestic material was recovered from the fills of the ditches which replaced the earlier post-built structures and pits. This included residual finds which may have been associated with the earlier features.

MATERIAL FROM THE BOUNDARY DITCH, STRUCTURE 4

The ceramic assemblage

A very large assemblage of pottery was recovered from the fills of the boundary ditch (S4; 41 EVEs/42961g). This assemblage represents 46.9% by EVEs and 39% by weight of the total stratified pottery from LD76. In general this assemblage differs from much of the rest of the pottery: the average sherd size is larger and less abraded, and there are many complete profiles. There are sherd links between all three layers of the ditch. There is relatively little residuality within this assemblage, with the major industries of the 1st and 2nd centuries at

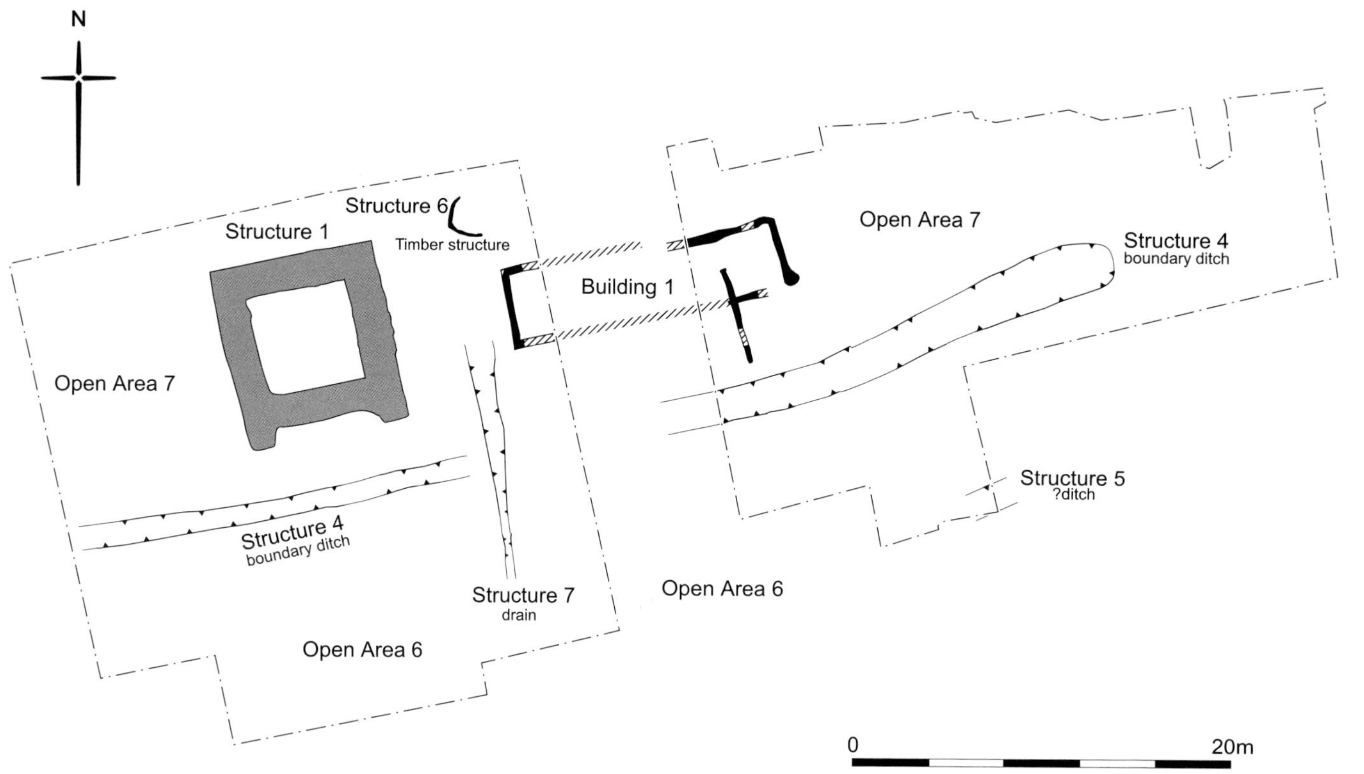

Fig 9 3rd-century intensification of land use, period 3, phase 6 (scale 1:400)

Verulamium and Highgate represented, but only in small quantities. The majority of the pottery dates to the mid 3rd century. Independent dating evidence is also provided by several coins found within the fills (see below).

The ditch (S4) was excavated in sections, with the fills from the western part of the ditch split into lower and upper fills (Fig 6). The nature of the surviving record did not, however, allow the fills from the eastern end of the ditch (where the majority of the pottery was located) to be separated in the same way. In addition, later layers slumping into the ditch may not have been identified during excavation and a small amount of intrusive material seems to have been introduced into the ditch assemblage. As a consequence the material from this feature should be treated with some caution.

The pottery from the upper fills is a comparatively small group and is dated by a coin of AD 270–90 in LD76 [253]. Dating evidence for the lower fills consists of a coin dated AD 270–85 in LD76 [288], while for the eastern fills there are coins in LD76 [146] dated AD 332–4, and in LD76 [357] dated AD 324–8. Overall the latest samian is dated to the second quarter of the 3rd century. The latest coarse ware is one example of a Portchester 'D' ware jar (PORD 2) in LD76 [217]. This is the only sherd and there are no examples of the other diagnostically 4th-century fabric, 'calcite-gritted' ware (CALC) and so it is possible that this PORD sherd is intrusive. Tables 7–8 present the pottery data for Structure 4 as a whole. A representative selection of vessels from the ditch has been illustrated (<P8>–<P33>, Figs 14–15; <SAM43>, <SAM47>, Fig 19; <SAM50>, <SAM52>, <SAM55>, <SAM57>, Fig 20; <SAM59>, <SAM62>, <SAM65>, Fig 21).

Pottery fabrics

The most common reduced ware in the assemblage is BB1, while AHFA is only present in very small quantities. Similar proportions are seen in a group from Leadenhall Court, dated to AD 230–50/60 (Symonds and Tomber 1991, 71–3) and in a large assemblage from a well at 10–18 Union Street, Southwark (18.56 EVEs/18476g), dated to *c* AD 250–70 (BB1 31.3% by EVEs/30.6% by weight and AHFA 13.4%/10.6%; Seeley in prep). The most common fine ware is Nene Valley colour-coated ware. There are only two records for the later Romano-British fine ware OXRC which is dated from *c* AD 270 in London. The high value for North Kent white-slipped ware is due to the presence of a complete rim from a disc-necked flagon (NKWS 1L; <P9>, Fig 14).

The high percentage of samian (8.5% weight), especially East Gaulish, distinguishes this from other assemblages in London of this period. The 10–18 Union Street well group, which in other respects is similar to this assemblage, only contains 2.9% (EVEs)/2.0% (weight) of East Gaulish Samian (SAMEG). Other imported fine wares at Shadwell include Moselkeramik (MOSL) and Cologne colour-coated (KOLN). Sourced amphora fabrics include the Pélichet 47/Dressel 30 (GAUL1) and the late North African (NAFR) fabrics. Baetican Dressel 20 amphora is the single most common type of amphora (BAET 8DR20). Other imports include Rhineland white ware (RHWW), North Gaulish grey ware and white ware (NGGW, NGWH). The late imported fabrics such as Mayen ware (MAYEN) and Speicher ware (SPEC) are noticeably absent from the assemblage.

Pottery forms

Everted-rimmed jars occur mostly in BB1. Both illustrated examples have obtuse lattice decoration with a faint burnished

Table 7 Pottery fabric quantities from Structure 4

Ware group	Fabric	Rows	% rows	EVEs	% EVEs	Weight (g)	% weight
Amphorae	AMPH	8	1.5	0	–	687	1.6
	AMPH1	2	0.4	0	–	64	0.1
	AMPH2	4	0.8	0	–	277	0.6
	AMPH3	9	1.7	0	–	2230	5.2
	AMPH4	1	0.2	0	–	142	0.3
	BAET	16	3.0	0	–	4516	10.5
	GAUL1	21	4.0	0.2	0.5	2073	4.8
	NAFR	5	0.9	0	–	636	1.5
	NAFR1	1	0.2	0	–	12	<0.1
Samian ware	SAM	2	0.4	0	–	57	0.1
	SAMCG	29	5.5	0.71	1.7	578	1.3
	SAMEG	57	10.8	4.33	10.4	2974	6.9
	SAMLG	6	1.1	0	–	31	0.1
	CGBL	1	0.2	0	–	2	<0.1
Imported fine ware	KOLN	16	3.0	1.69	4.1	787	1.8
	MOSL	29	5.5	1.08	2.6	490	1.1
Romano-British fine ware	NVCC	95	17.9	10.3	24.9	5752	13.4
	MICA	1	0.2	0.08	0.2	5	<0.1
Black-burnished type ware	BB1	85	16.0	11.9	28.6	12052	28.1
	BB2	8	1.5	0.9	2.2	480	1.1
	BBS	5	0.9	0.61	1.5	383	0.9
Reduced ware	FINE	2	0.4	0	–	17	<0.1
	AHFA	1	0.2	0.15	0.4	18	<0.1
	HWC	1	0.2	0.2	0.5	11	<0.1
	NGGW	2	0.4	0.2	0.5	18	<0.1
	SAND	33	6.2	0.61	1.5	973	2.3
	SAND1	9	1.7	2.67	6.4	1646	3.8
Oxidised ware	OXRC	2	0.4	0	–	46	0.1
	NGWH	7	1.3	0.1	0.2	41	0.1
	NKWS	4	0.8	1	2.4	195	0.5
	OXWW	7	1.3	0.31	0.7	590	1.4
	PORD	1	0.2	0	–	5	<0.1
	RHWW	3	0.6	0.33	0.8	1355	3.2
	RWS	1	0.2	0	–	24	0.1
	OXID	38	7.2	3.34	8.0	2177	5.1
	VRW	13	2.5	0.81	1.9	1579	3.7
Miscellaneous ware	CC	5	0.9	0.08	0.2	38	0.1
Totals		**530**	**100.0**	**41.62**	**100.0**	**42961**	**100.0**

See Table 2 for key to fabric codes
Rows: on the Oracle database, each line (row) consists of a unique fabric, form and decoration combination
EVEs: estimated vessel equivalents

Table 8 Pottery form quantities from Structure 4

Form	Code	Rows	% rows	EVEs	% EVEs	Weight (g)	% weight
Uncertain	–	61	11.5	0.1	0.2	1983	4.6
Flagon	1	11	2.1	2.32	5.6	946	2.2
	1B7/9	1	0.2	0.4	1.0	270	0.6
	1D	1	0.2	1	2.4	32	0.1
Jar	2	43	8.1	1.92	4.6	2529	5.9
	2/3	2	0.4	0	–	75	0.2
	2A17	3	0.6	0.64	1.5	109	0.3
	2F	8	1.5	1.55	3.7	616	1.4
	2F13	1	0.2	0.15	0.4	29	0.1
	2FX	1	0.2	0.22	0.5	95	0.2
	2H	1	0.2	0.45	1.1	531	1.2
	2J	1	0.2	0.11	0.3	19	<0.1
	2R	1	0.2	1	2.4	46	0.1
	2T	4	0.8	0.82	2.0	340	0.8
Beaker	3	127	24.0	12.6	30.3	6285	14.6
	3K	10	1.9	0.54	1.3	511	1.2
	3L	7	1.3	0.1	0.2	41	0.1
Bowl	4/5	30	5.7	0.26	0.6	3753	8.7
	4A	1	0.2	0.12	0.3	78	0.2
	4DR29	2	0.4	0	–	5	<0.1
	4DR30	2	0.4	0	–	15	<0.1
	4DR30/37	3	0.6	0.22	0.5	85	0.2
	4DR37	23	4.3	1.24	3.0	1127	2.6
	4DR38	9	1.7	1.21	2.9	576	1.3
	4G	2	0.4	0.2	0.5	49	0.1
	4G226	9	1.7	2.23	5.4	1560	3.6
	4H	6	1.1	0.9	2.2	381	0.9
	4M	12	2.3	2.9	7.0	3498	8.1
	4Q	1	0.2	0	–	27	0.1
Plate/dish	5	3	0.6	0.35	0.8	579	1.3
	5CU15	1	0.2	0	–	77	0.2
	5DR18	2	0.4	0	–	9	<0.1
	5DR18/31	2	0.4	0.12	0.3	43	0.1
	5DR31	5	0.9	0.48	1.2	168	0.4
	5DR31R	8	1.5	0	–	518	1.2
	5DR32	8	1.5	1.17	2.8	409	1.0
	5DR36	1	0.2	0	–	7	<0.1
	5J	18	3.4	4.44	10.7	2495	5.8
Cup	6DR33	9	1.7	0.5	1.2	119	0.3
Mortarium	7	13	2.5	0.18	0.4	1719	4.0
	7DR45	2	0.4	0	–	57	0.1
	7HAM	1	0.2	0.15	0.4	253	0.6
	7M17	1	0.2	0.2	0.5	236	0.5
	7M22	1	0.2	0.11	0.3	64	0.1
Amphora	8	29	5.5	0	–	3906	9.1
	8DR20	16	3.0	0	–	4516	10.5
	8G	21	4.0	0.2	0.5	2073	4.8
Box/lid	9A	1	0.2	0	–	32	0.1
	9G	4	0.8	0.34	0.8	46	0.1
	9GL	1	0.2	0.18	0.4	24	0.1
Totals		**530**	**100.0**	**41.62**	**100.0**	**42961**	**100.0**

See Table 3 for key to form codes
Rows: on the Oracle database, each line (row) consists of a unique fabric, form and decoration combination
EVEs: estimated vessel equivalents

line above, delineating the decorated zone (<P10> and <P12>, Fig 14). The rims do not flare beyond the girth of the vessel. The most notable feature of the assemblage is the dominance of the beaker form (15.9% weight), which most frequently occurs in the fabric NVCC. When this assemblage was quantified, the typology used by the Museum of London for Roman pottery (Marsh and Tyers 1979) had not been extended to include the late beaker forms. The quantified data do not therefore show the true proportions between bag-shaped (3J), necked globular (3K) and pentice (3L) beakers. Only where a reference was given in the original records to a publication has the beaker been identified as a specific form. Two of the illustrated bag-shaped beakers in NVCC (<P16> and <P19>, Fig 14) are decorated with underslip barbotine scroll decoration. In the most recent overview of the products of the Nene Valley pottery industry these vessels are dated to the mid 3rd century (Perrin 1999, 93, fig 60, nos 143–50). An unusual form of decoration occurs on another bag-shaped beaker (<P18>, Fig 14) which has underslip diagonal barbotine lines. Production of the necked beakers with scale decoration (<P21> and <P22>, Fig 14) is thought to start in the second quarter of the 3rd century (ibid, 94, fig 61, nos 165–6). Two examples have been illustrated from the range of sizes present in the assemblage. The imported beakers occur in MOSL, KOLN and North Gaulish white ware (NGWH) and all have parallels in examples from the waterfront assemblage at St Magnus House (Richardson 1986). The MOSL beakers are mostly necked beakers with round indentations (<P13>, Fig 14) although one 'motto beaker' is also present (<P15>, Fig 14). The decorative scheme on the illustrated KOLN bag-shaped beaker (<P14>, Fig 14) is very similar to an example at St Magnus House (ibid, 112–13, fig 1.84). The NGWH sherds are all from rouletted pentice beakers; none were suitable for illustration but again these have parallels in examples at St Magnus House (ibid, 106–7, fig 1.43).

Within this assemblage, the Drag 37 bowl form is the commonest samian form. Most of the bowls and dishes are the black-burnished ware forms – flanged bowls (4M), incipient-flanged bowls (4G226) and plain-rimmed dishes (5J). These forms occur mostly in BB1 although they are also present in the unsourced sand-tempered fabric (SAND1) and black-burnished style ware (BBS). These forms within this assemblage are invariably decorated with intersecting arcs on the exterior and curvilinear decoration on the base (<P24> and <P28>, Fig 15). The plain-rimmed dish (<P28>, Fig 15) has wide intersecting arcs and a slightly sagging base; it is almost identical to an example from the waterfront group at St Magnus House (Richardson 1986, 125, fig 1.164). Two examples occur of the handled oval 'fish' dish (<P27>, Fig 15); these are dated from the mid 3rd century (Holbrook and Bidwell 1991, 113, fig 33, no. 61.1). The flanged bowls (<P24>–<P26>, Fig 15) all have extended flanges rather than the smaller flanges seen on later 4th-century forms usually occurring in AHFA fabric, as at Great Dover Street (Seeley 2000, 55, fig 40, nos P50 and P52) and Billingsgate Bath House (Symonds and Tomber 1991, 77, fig 14, nos 148–9). At Exeter this type of flanged bowl is generally dated from *c* AD 270 but they may occur earlier (Holbrook and Bidwell 1991, 98–9, fig 31, no. 45).

Mortaria are not well represented in the assemblage. Oxfordshire white ware (OXWW) mortaria occur in Young forms M17 and M22 (Young 1977, fig 21, nos M17.1–11, and fig 23, M22.1–20). The Rhineland white ware (RHWW) late walled mortarium (<P30>, Fig 15) resembles vessels at St Magnus House (Richardson 1986, 112, fig 1.78–80). An unusual form and fabric combination is the oxidised ware castor box (OXID 9G ROD; <P33>, Fig 15). Castor boxes are rare in London and are usually in the fine ware fabric NVCC, whereas this vessel is in a relatively coarse oxidised ware.

The dating of the non-samian pottery assemblage from the boundary ditch is problematic. In general 3rd-century pottery groups are not well understood (Symonds and Tomber 1991, 60) and the dating for this assemblage is made more difficult by the presence of possibly intrusive material. The samian is dated to *c* AD 225–50 and many of the non-samian forms and fabrics have parallels in the earlier assemblage at St Magnus House. Most of the forms, especially the NVCC beakers, could pre-date AD 250. The group contains, however, black-burnished forms such as flanged bowls and later everted-rimmed jars, which do occur in London pre-AD 250 but tend to be more common after that date. The abundance of flanged bowls in particular may be an indicator of a post-AD 250 date for this assemblage. Additionally, the low percentages of OXRC as well as AHFA, if they are contemporary with the rest of the group, suggest the date is post-AD 250, for these fabrics rarely occur before this date.

Glass and accessioned finds

A quantity of glass vessels were also found in the boundary ditch (S4; <G4>, <G30>, <G33>, <G36>–<G62>, Fig 24). The same group produced an enamelled circular plate brooch (<S1>, Fig 25) which dates from the 2nd century and is thus residual. This ditch also produced coins of late 3rd- and 4th-century date (see above, p16) and several fragmentary bone hairpins (<S7>, <S10> and <S11>), though none ascribable to a specific type. There are in addition some poorly preserved and unidentifiable fragments of copper alloy and iron.

Animal bone

A total of 292 fragments (8.326kg) of animal bone was recovered from the boundary ditch (S4) The assemblages were again dominated by cattle and cattle-sized fragments (see S4, Table 15), represented by a mix of skeletal parts (S4, Table 16), with the fragments largely composed of vertebrae and ribs. This ditch contained sheep/goat and pig, also showing a mixed distribution of parts. A single goat bone was from a very young individual, comparable with the period 5 cattle example in showing the presence locally of stock rearing or keeping.

There is a noticeably high proportion of horse bone, with a variety of skeletal parts, none of which appeared to have been in articulation when found. The few which could be aged and/or measured suggest that these animals were adult and relatively short. All the horse bones are badly eroded and highly fragmented, which suggests that their depositional history was different (discussed in Chapter 5.8). There is, however, a single case of butchery, a knife cut on a horse femur shaft, which is clearly a defleshing mark. While this butchery indicates that horseflesh was at least occasionally consumed, it does not provide unequivocal evidence for human consumption of such meat, it perhaps being fed to dogs.

Building 1: rectilinear timber building

The rectilinear building (B1) straddled both sites and was clearly substantial, being 4.0m wide and 15.0m long. It was evidently built of timber and set on a sill beam in a shallow earth-fast foundation. A structural cut contained an East Gaulish Samian (SAMEG) Drag 31/Lud Sa bowl, dated to the later second–mid 3rd century. The form of the foundation suggests that the building was open on its southern side; a further T-shaped timber slot was noted at the south-east corner of the building and may have formed part of it. A small patch of brickearth flooring at the south-west corner of the building was the only surviving evidence of any associated internal surfaces. The associated finds gave no indication of its function. However, its large size and unusual form (lack of obvious internal partitions and open to the south) might suggest that it was used as a shed, barn or similar non-domestic building. The very few finds in the building were a coin LD76 [310] dated *c* AD 270–85 and three glass vessel fragments <G10>, <G73> and <G81>. Building 1 also yielded five fragments of animal bone (just 0.028kg), including both cattle-sized and sheep-sized fragments (B1, Table 15).

Structure 6: wattle structure

The semi-circular structure (S6) which lay to the north-west of Building 1 consisted of a wattle fence set in a shallow foundation trench. Within this structure lay a deposit of pottery and charcoal which might indicate its use for cooking, although the available description of the feature does not particularly suggest that there was a hearth or oven. The pottery included a SAMEG decorated bowl dating from the later second to mid 3rd century.

Structure 7: north–south drain

The north–south aligned drain (S7) which ran through the apparent gap in Structure 4 lay *c* 1.0m to the west of Building 1. The drain was timber lined and was thought by the excavator originally to have terminated at its northern end in a tank similar to that noted in the later industrial phase, although all traces of such a feature had been destroyed by later truncation. The drain seems also to have been truncated at its southern end; it may be assumed that it once ran to the southern limit of the site, as did the later drains.

Discussion of phase 6

The nature of the land-use change indicated by this phase is not clear. The similarity between the timber-lined drain and the later industrial features might suggest that this phase represents a precursor to the subsequent clearly industrial use of the site. If this was the case, then Building 1 may have been a workshop or shed, as suggested by its form. The reason behind a change from fences to ditches as a means of defining the site is not obvious; perhaps it was linked to an increasing concern with drainage inferred from the proliferation of ditches, drains and gullies from this phase onwards.

Once again the dating of the phase is uncertain. A small quantity of late second- to mid 3rd-century samian was recovered from the disuse backfills of Building 1. The external deposits to the west of Building 1 contained samian of Hadrianic to mid 3rd-century date. The timber drain contained samian of 2nd-century date only. The ditches (S4 and S5) on LD76 contained samian of Antonine to mid 3rd-century date but also yielded coins dated to AD 332–3 and AD 324–8 and a non-samian pottery assemblage datable to *c* AD 250–70 (excluding a single sherd of PORD). Likewise the ditch (S4) on LD74 contained no samian but did yield a coin [F17] dated to AD 259–68. The divergence between a samian assemblage of early to mid 3rd-century date, a non-samian assemblage of late 3rd-century date and coins of the 4th century is problematic.

One of the ditches (S4) produced a large and varied finds assemblage. It contained nearly half the pottery (by EVEs) from the site and in general differs from much of the rest of the pottery: the average sherd size is larger and less abraded, and there are a substantial number of complete profiles. This group is exceptional in its size and by having a high percentage of late samian which has no parallel in contemporary assemblages from inland London sites. The assemblage does contain vessels which exhibit signs of use. However, beyond these observations it is not possible to define further the function of this assemblage, especially as it cannot be related directly to any of the buildings on the site including the masonry structure. The fills of the ditch also produced 40% (by fragment count) of the animal bone from LD76 including 75% of the horse bones and nearly all the dog bones. Two nearly complete glass vessels (G<30>, <G36>–<G62>) also come from the ditch and their good survival may indicate that they were nearly complete when they were originally deposited.

Phase 7: disuse of Building 1 and replacement ditches

The disuse of the timber building (B1) and associated structures is marked by the infilling of the east–west aligned ditches and their replacement with less substantial gullies (phase 7, Fig 10) in Open Area 8. These gullies truncate the north–south aligned drain. A number of slots, gullies or pits also truncated the foundations of Building 1 indicating that it went out of use in this phase. The animal bone assemblage recovered from these gullies (OA8; 71 fragments, 0.886kg) was notable for the large proportion of the cattle bones, similar to the pitfill assemblages in Open Area 5, composed of head and feet parts. Of the 32 fragments, 17 were head and feet parts, increasing to 26 if loose teeth are included (Table 16). These figures suggest a particular type of waste such as from butchery or an industrial process, as well as showing, from the loose teeth, the high level of fragmentation.

The gullies which replaced the earlier ditches follow a similar alignment – on LD76 in one case, they were cut into the upper fills of the preceding ditch – but were much shallower and narrower (500mm wide and *c* 400mm deep on average). Two sets of gullies are represented, stretching across both LD74 and LD76. The northernmost gully (S8) had an apparently irregularly-rounded terminus at its western end (Fig 6) and

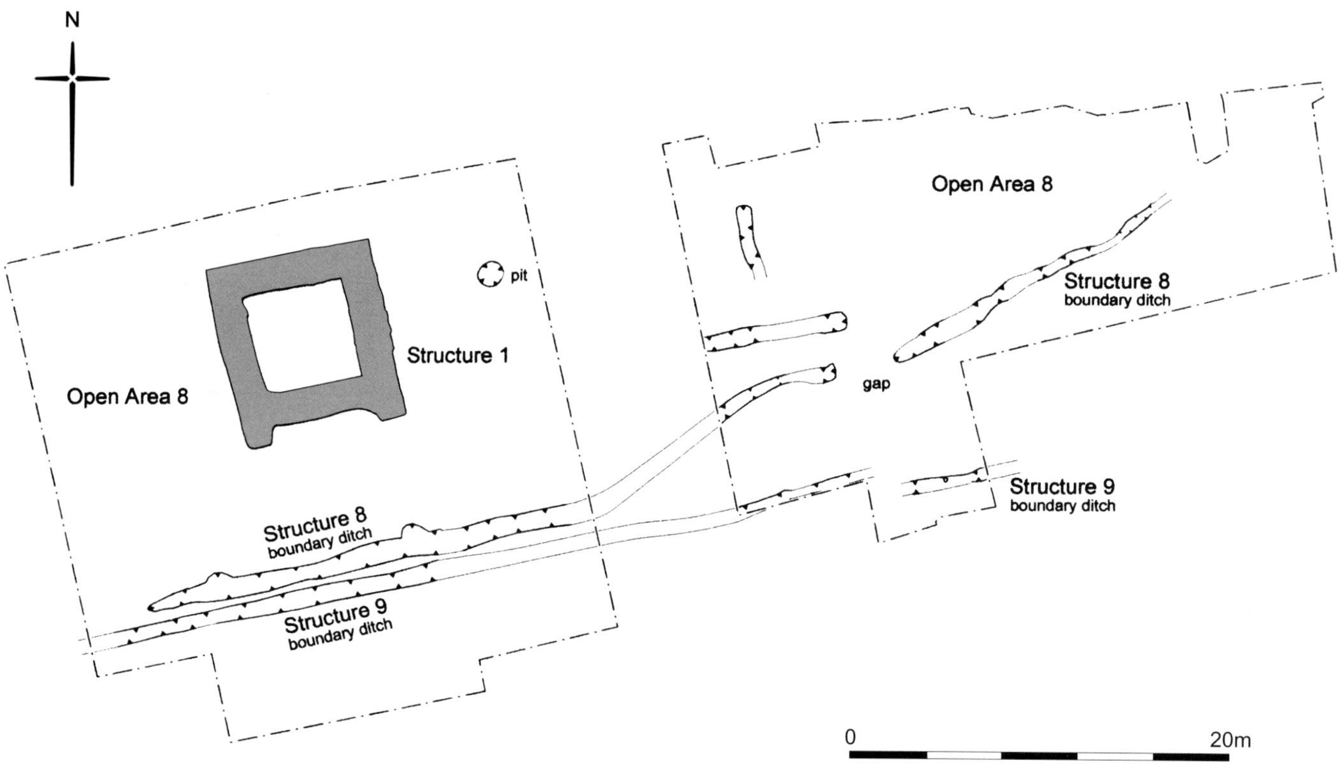

Fig 10 Replacement ditches and disuse of Building 1, period 3, phase 7 (scale 1:400)

closely followed the alignment of the earlier fence line (S2), before in its eastern part turning north-eastwards and closely following the course of the earlier ditch (S4). The eastern end of the gully was not seen owing to truncation by later features. In the western part of LD76 lay a 3.0m-wide gap in the gully, marked by rounded and partly expanded terminals. The fill of this gully contained 4th-century coins, fragmentary bone pins, part of a copper alloy spoon (<S20>, Fig 25) and glassware (<G3>, <G35> and <G63>, Fig 24). A large pottery assemblage was found in the fill of this gully weighing 9506g, 8.69 EVEs (S8, Tables 9–10). The proportions of fabrics present can be compared with those from the boundary ditch (S4, Tables 7–8).

AHFA and BB1 are now present in almost equal quantities and OXRC is also more common. NVCC is still the dominant fabric and fine ware measured by EVEs. Samian, both Central and East Gaulish, is still present in the assemblage but in much lower quantities and by this period it is residual. PORD and CALC are both present in small quantities, indicating a mid 4th-century date. This date is also indicated by the presence of several AHFA bowls with a small flange. This variant of the flanged bowl (4M) is a type 6C.1 (Lyne and Jeffries 1979, 49, fig 38, no. 6C.1) and is dated to AD 330–420. The coins in this assemblage are dated to AD 330–46 and AD 330–5. The high proportion by EVEs of North Gaulish white ware is due to the presence of a complete rim of a pentice beaker (NGWH 3L). Similar beakers in this fabric come from the large waterfront group at St Magnus House (Richardson 1986, 107, no. 1.43). Structure 8 also contained an East Gaulish samian sherd which has fine post-firing grooves on both sides. One suggestion is that it might have been reused to sharpen pins or needles.

The southern gully (S9) ran on an east–west alignment, across both LD74 and LD76 and apparently extended beyond the limits of excavation to both east and west (Fig 6). The fills of this gully yielded one coin dated AD 347–8 and unidentified copper alloy fragments. Two of the fills, LD76 [1097] and [1098], contained PORD suggesting a mid to late 4th-century date. Sherds from two of the decorated samian Drag 37 bowls were found in both gullies (S8 and S9, <SAM42>, Fig 19; <SAM49>, Fig 20)

The two gullies, Structures 8 and 9, produced relatively small quantities of animal bone, 47 fragments (0.669kg) and 11 fragments (0.565kg) respectively (S8 and S9, Table 15). These features again contained a rather narrow species range dominated by cattle and cattle-sized fragments. Similarly, the major species share a wide distribution of skeletal parts, as shown in Structure 8. There is a continuation of local stock rearing, shown by the presence of the scapula of a very young sheep. The three horse bones within these features were all severely eroded. One of these bones is actually two tarsals which have fused together. This could represent a case of spavin (after Baker and Brothwell 1980), which may in turn be related either to stress (of the ligaments) or to a severe concussion of the joint. In general, this condition would cause only a relatively mild degree of lameness.

Two further cut features truncated the foundation beam slots of Building 1 on LD76. These features were both wider and deeper than the contemporary gullies, with steeper-sided profiles. Both features seem to have been rather shorter than the contemporary gullies to the south, one being *c* 4.0m long and the other between 7.0m and 15m long. A shallow circular pit truncated the north-western corner of Building 1. The

Table 9 Pottery fabric quantities from Structure 8

Ware group	Fabric	Rows	% rows	EVEs	% EVEs	Weight (g)	% weight
Amphorae	AMPH	3	2.1	0	–	196	2.1
	AMPH1	1	0.7	0	–	8	0.1
	AMPH3	1	0.7	0	–	92	1.0
	BAET	3	2.1	0	–	471	5.0
	GAUL1	3	2.1	0	–	110	1.2
	NAFR	1	0.7	0	–	50	0.5
	NAFR1	1	0.7	0	–	299	3.1
Samian ware	SAM	1	0.7	0	–	16	0.2
	SAMCG	6	4.3	0	–	49	0.5
	SAMEG	4	2.8	0.15	1.7	91	1.0
Imported fine ware	CGBL	1	0.7	0	–	3	<0.1
	EPON	1	0.7	0	–	1	<0.1
	KOLN	3	2.1	0.1	1.2	43	0.5
	MOSL	7	5.0	0.23	2.6	47	0.5
Romano-British fine ware	NVCC	24	17.0	2.43	28.0	1015	10.7
	MICA	1	0.7	0.25	2.9	78	0.8
	OXRC	6	4.3	0.2	2.3	347	3.7
Black-burnished type ware	BB1	12	8.5	1.03	11.9	1331	14.0
	BB2	1	0.7	0.07	0.8	17	0.2
	BBS	4	2.8	0.3	3.5	329	3.5
Reduced ware	AHFA	8	5.7	0.78	9.0	826	8.7
	SAND	20	14.2	1.43	16.5	1632	17.2
	SAND1	1	0.7	0.03	0.3	79	0.8
	COAR	1	0.7	0	–	15	0.2
	CALC	1	0.7	0	–	60	0.6
Oxidised ware	NGWH	1	0.7	1	11.5	136	1.4
	OXPA	1	0.7	0	–	3	<0.1
	OXWW	3	2.1	0.15	1.7	297	3.1
	PORD	2	1.4	0.1	1.2	49	0.5
	RHWW	1	0.7	0.1	1.2	555	5.8
	RWS	1	0.7	0	–	3	<0.1
	OXID	7	5.0	0.14	1.6	383	4.0
	VRW	2	1.4	0	–	106	1.1
Miscellaneous	CC	8	5.7	0.2	2.3	769	8.1
Totals		**141**	**100.0**	**8.69**	**100.0**	**9506**	**100.0**

See Table 2 for key to fabric codes
Rows: on the Oracle database, each line (row) consists of a unique fabric, form and decoration combination
EVEs: estimated vessel equivalents

Table 10 Pottery form quantities from Structure 8

Form	Code	Rows	% rows	EVEs	% EVEs	Weight (g)	% weight
Uncertain	-	18	12.8	0	–	636	6.7
Flagon	1	2	1.4	0.25	2.9	688	7.2
Jar	2	16	11.3	0.66	7.6	1117	11.8
	2F	1	0.7	0.2	2.3	52	0.5
	2FX	2	1.4	0.22	2.5	131	1.4
	2T	3	2.1	0.4	4.6	90	0.9
	2V	3	2.1	0.1	1.2	514	5.4
	2W	1	0.7	0.1	1.2	34	0.4
Beaker	3	31	22.0	1.61	18.5	850	8.9
	3J	2	1.4	0.95	10.9	201	2.1
	3K	4	2.8	0.2	2.3	192	2.0
	3L	3	2.1	1.2	13.8	149	1.6
Bowl	4	2	1.4	0	–	196	2.1
	4/5	11	7.8	0.33	3.8	1337	14.1
	4CU21	1	0.7	0	–	4	<0.1
	4DR37	3	2.1	0	–	77	0.8
	4DR38	3	2.1	0	–	115	1.2
	4H	1	0.7	0.07	0.8	17	0.2
	4M	7	5.0	1.25	14.4	575	6.0
	4P24	1	0.7	0	–	60	0.6
Plate/dish	5DR31	1	0.7	0	–	19	0.2
	5J	5	3.5	0.75	8.6	276	2.9
Cup	6DR33	2	1.4	0.15	1.7	11	0.1
Mortarium	7	3	2.1	0.1	1.2	632	6.6
	7M22	1	0.7	0.15	1.7	220	2.3
Amphora	8	7	5.0	0	–	645	6.8
	8DR20	3	2.1	0	–	471	5.0
	8G	3	2.1	0	–	110	1.2
Box/lid	9A	1	0.7	0	–	87	0.9
Totals		**141**	**100.0**	**8.69**	**100.0**	**9506**	**100.0**

See Table 3 for key to form codes
Rows: on the Oracle database, each line (row) consists of a unique fabric, form and decoration combination
EVEs: estimated vessel equivalents

pottery from these features is dated from the later 3rd century by the presence of OXRC. Other forms and fabrics present, more common from the second half of the 3rd century, included NVCC pentice beakers and flanged bowls, MOSL beakers, a SAMEG Drag 37 bowl and BB1 plain-rimmed dishes and flanged bowls. The coins are dated to AD 270–80 in LD76 [268] and AD 270–85 in LD76 [255] and [256].

It would seem that these gullies represented continued use of the earlier landscape divisions. It is notable that the fills of almost all the features belonging to this phase contained substantial quantities of demolition material and in particular charcoal, burnt clay and daub, as well as smaller amounts of stone. The quantity of material seems to be too large and too widely spread to have been derived solely from the demolition of Building 1; the demolition material may also have been derived partly from the destruction of nearby buildings and structures, some of which must have been, in part at least, constructed of stone. The obvious immediate source of such material is the stone 'tower' (S1), although it is possible that other, probably clay and timber, buildings lay beyond the limits of excavation.

The finds from this phase included notable quantities of 3rd-century coins and pottery (although the latest coins from the fills of the two gullies are datable to later than AD 340, apparently indicating either a high degree of residuality in the finds assemblage or later contamination). These finds were presumably deposited as the gullies went out of use and seem to indicate that the gullies were only in use for a short time, the previous phase also being datable to the late 3rd century.

2.4 Period 4: mid 4th-century industrial activity

Phase 8: timber-lined tanks, drains and metalling

Open Area 9: soil accumulation

This phase is marked by a complete change in the apparent use of the site and a sweeping away of the previous landscape divisions. These divisions, established earlier – possibly as early as the 2nd century – and perpetuated in successive fence, ditch and gully lines, were no longer maintained. Instead a number of timber-lined tanks and associated drains and metalled surfaces were constructed in Open Area 9, cutting across and obscuring the earlier divisions. All of these features were observed on LD74; there appears not to have been any contemporary activity on LD76. The form of these features suggests that they had an industrial function (Fig 11).

Structures 10–12: timber-lined tanks

Three distinct structures were noted. One lay at the eastern edge of LD74 (S10) and was composed of a bipartite clay- and timber-lined tank with a timber-lined drain leading from its southern edge to the southern limit of excavation (Fig 6). The tank was approximately 3.0m wide, divided into two equal parts by a clay partition. Both east and west portions of the tank seem to have been wood lined; the western part was additionally lined with clay around the sides but not the base. The drain led southwards from the western, clay-lined, portion of the tank. The drain seems to have been intended to capture the overflow from the tank since it leaves the top of the tank. The drain was timber lined and seems to have consisted of two phases. It is possible that the bipartite construction of the tank reflects two phases of construction for the entire feature.

A circular, timber-lined tank (S11) lay in the southern central part of LD74. The feature was *c* 1.0m in diameter and may have been barrel lined since traces of vertical timbers were noted on the sides, and the base also preserved traces of wood. No drains were associated with this feature.

A small, square, timber-lined tank (S12) lay close to the southern limit of excavation. This tank, approximately 0.80m^2, had been vertically truncated by a later feature, but the lowest three sets of planking survived to a height of 0.50m. The planks were set horizontally and were dovetailed at the corners. The tank was set in a construction cut which was lined with clay. Five stakeholes, arranged in an L-shape around the north and east sides of the tank, may also have been associated with this feature, defining the construction cut or supporting a superstructure. Two drains were associated with the tank; the exact nature of the relationship had been removed by a later feature which truncated the upper part of the tank and its surroundings. Both drains were timber lined; one ran southwards from a point just west of the tank and the other ran westwards from the tank. The drains both also sloped away from the tank, suggesting that they were overflow rather than feeder drains. The leather briefs (LD74 <383>, Figs 12 and 27) and a shoe sole were found in the backfill of the tank.

An area of gravel metalling lay to the north and west of these features, continuing for a short distance to the east of the drain leading from Structure 10.

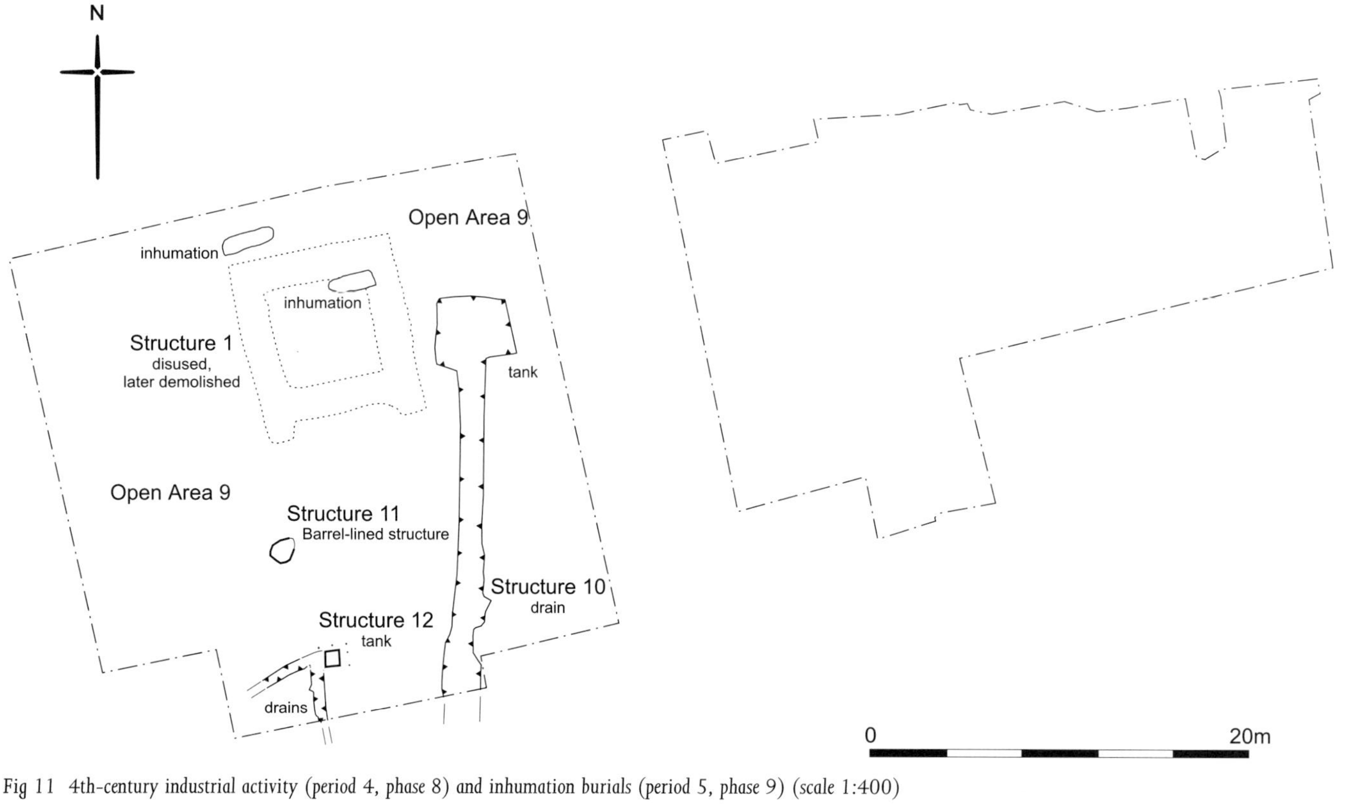

Fig 11 4th-century industrial activity (period 4, phase 8) and inhumation burials (period 5, phase 9) (scale 1:400)

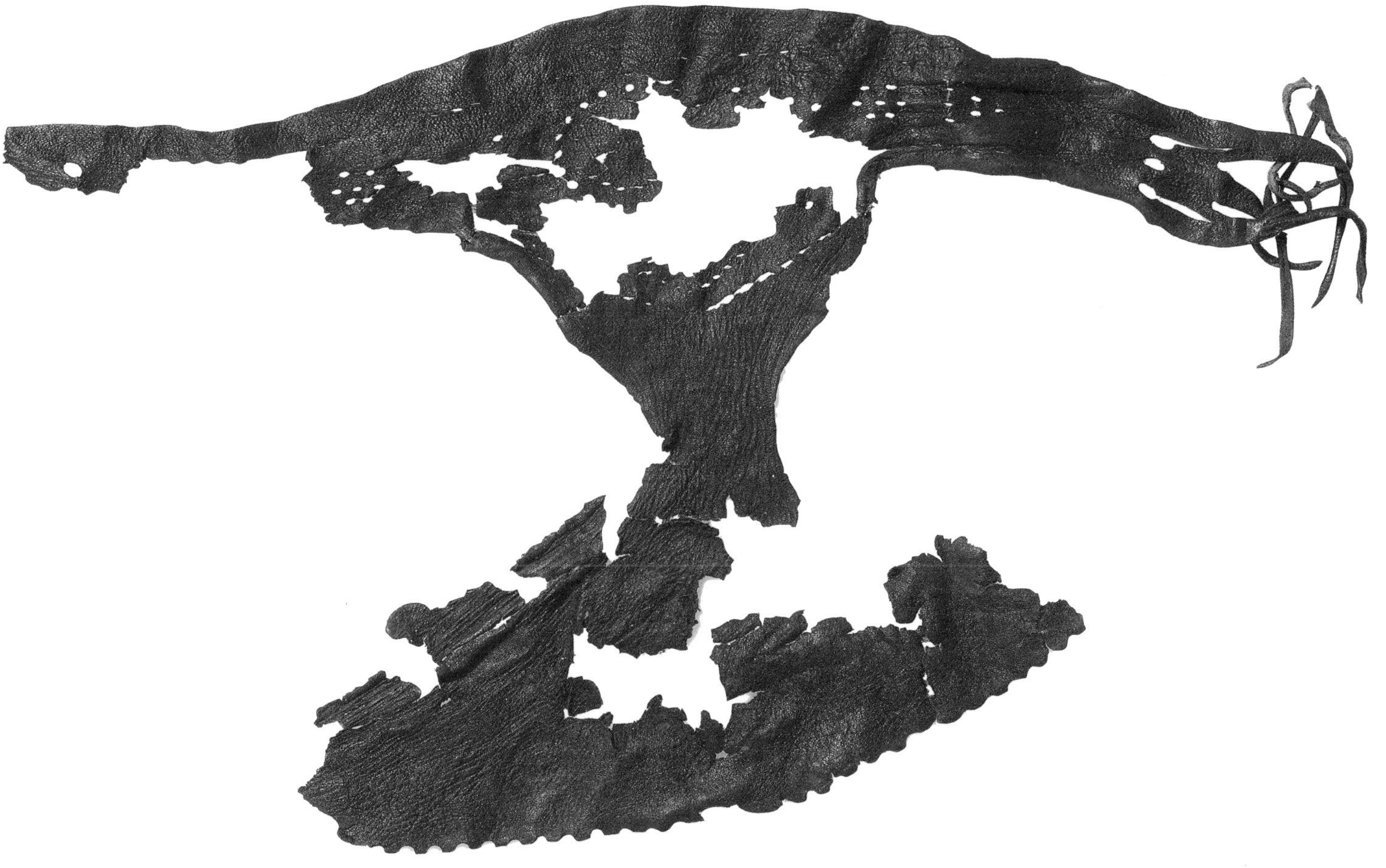

Fig 12 Leather 'bikini' or briefs LD74 <383> (reconstructed hip width c 400mm including shrinkage) (scale 1:2)

The form of these features strongly suggests an industrial function. The waterproof lining of some of the features and the apparent concern with drainage indicates an industry involving the use of liquid, such as tanning. The presence of two leather items, which included the leather briefs, in the backfill of Structure 12, is, however, likely to represent domestic rubbish disposal, unrelated to any earlier use of the tanks. Without further evidence from waste materials or environmental data the function of these structures must remain uncertain.

These features contained substantial quantities of residual 3rd-century material. However, the latest coin dates were AD 340–6 and AD 350–6 from Structure 10 and AD 347–8 from Structure 12; from the gravel metalling the coins were unspecific 3rd/4th century in date. This phase should, therefore, be dated to about the third quarter of the 4th century or later. It is interpreted as an industrial phase, seen only at LD74, where the presence of timber-lined tanks may suggest that tanning was carried out. Apart from the leather briefs, none of the objects deposited in the tank were available for study. A ceramic mould <S27> found in Open Area 10 in the succeeding phase may have been associated with this industrial phase, although the date of the manufactured object, and indeed its form, are uncertain (see Chapter 5.5).

A large amount of samian was recovered from Open Area 9; although it includes some earlier forms, generally it is dated c AD 225–50.

2.5 Period 5: late 4th-century inhumation burials and the abandonment of the site

Phase 9: demolition deposit and inhumation burials

Open Area 10: demolition deposit

The disuse of the industrial structures (phase 9) is marked by a substantial deposit of masonry rubble over almost all of LD74 and over most of the western part of LD76, Open Area 10 (not illustrated). As well as mortar and chalk, the material from LD74 included (roof) tile, flue tiles and *opus signinum* indicating that it was probably derived from a domestic building; some of the material must, therefore, have come from beyond the limits of the study area. The large amount of ragstone/limestone in these deposits was most probably derived from Structure 1. The large quantity, mixed nature and wide scatter of this material seem to indicate deliberate demolition rather than gradual decay and it is, therefore, to this phase that the robbing of the western part of Structure 1 should be assigned.

The date at which Structure 1 was demolished and the industrial features were sealed by the resultant rubble seems from the coin evidence to have been in or after AD 365. Coins of this date were the latest to be recovered from the rubble deposits and from the backfill of the robbed foundations of Structure 1. The pottery assemblage from the redeposited destruction debris is small. Overall the pottery from Open Area 10 is dated later than previous groups by several sherds of PORD, the increased amount of OXRC and AHFA (the most common reduced ware) and a relatively low occurrence of BB1.

The reason for the deliberate demolition of the masonry structure and the subsequent use of the area is not clear. No structures have been identified postdating the deposition of the masonry rubble and so clearly, by then, any use of the site was less intensive than in previous phases.

INHUMATION BURIALS

An inhumation burial was inserted into the north–eastern corner of Structure 1 subsequent to its disuse. Neither this burial nor a second inhumation located immediately adjacent to the exterior of the north–western corner of the structure could be definitively dated (Fig 11). The external burial was extended, supine and east–west oriented. The burial within the structure seems to have been more disturbed. The proximity of the two burials to the masonry structure would seem not to be coincidental and may indicate a Roman rather than post-Roman date for their interment. If this date can be sustained then it might suggest that the site was being used once more as a cemetery, as it had been in the 2nd century. The paucity of available records from LD74 leaves open the possibility that the remains inside the structure had been redeposited and that the external burial should be assigned to phase 3.

A relatively substantial quantity of animal bones, 167 fragments (4.156kg), was recovered from Open Area 10 (Tables 15–16). This assemblage is very similar to those previously described, with a high count of cattle and cattle-sized fragments, and with cattle represented by a mixture of skeletal parts. Loose teeth are again relatively abundant, clearly showing a high level of fragmentation (OA10, Table 16). It is conceivable that this represents preservation bias, which might have acted against the recovery of smaller species; there is a notable absence of bird bones, although one fishbone was recovered. It is the only fishbone from this site, identified as a (butchered) cod skull fragment. A chopped horse femur suggests, as in phase 6 (S4) above, the consumption of horseflesh. A further horse bone, a phalange, had been severely gnawed.

Phase 10: disuse, soil accumulation

Open Area 11: soil accumulation

Traces were identified on both LD74 and LD76 of a dark silt deposit (phase 10, OA11, not illustrated) similar in nature to topsoil. This deposit seems to have been 200–300mm thick and contained quantities of Roman finds of all periods. The latest coins here are dated to AD 367–75. The silt was capped by up to 2.0m of post-medieval dumps and although it contained a number of intrusive post-medieval finds it seems probable that the deposit was originally of late Roman origin and marks the soil development which occurred when the site eventually went out of use. The finds from this phase include several post-medieval items, including clay tobacco pipes and glassware. The latest Roman coins date from the mid to late 4th century (AD 367–75). Several personal items could date from the later Roman period – shale bracelet fragments (<S16>–<S17>, Fig 25) and a jet hairpin (<S4>, Fig 25), though a fragment of copper alloy brooch (<S2>) dates from the 1st or 2nd century and tweezers <S19> are not closely datable. It is likely that the finds from this area have been mixed during post-Roman soil development.

Open Area 11 provided a minor collection of animal bones (OA11, Table 15). The animal bones recovered from the 'topsoil' amounted to 73 fragments or 1.199kg. This assemblage features a relatively small range of species, similar to the previous assemblage but with a majority of sheep/goat fragments, in sharp contrast to the ubiquitous dominance of cattle/cattle-sized fragments found elsewhere at this site. All three major domesticates are represented by a wide range of skeletal parts, with cattle and sheep/goat once again having a high count of loose teeth. The single horse bone, a femur, which was in a relatively poor condition, had been butchered, so providing further evidence for the use of horsemeat.

3

Discussion

The Shadwell sites have previously attracted archaeological attention because of the initial interpretation of the masonry structure (S1) as a signal tower, on the basis of its form, location and visibility (Johnson 1975, 280). It is now clear that the stratigraphic sequence at Shadwell was much longer and more complex than the interim excavation notices suggested, diluting any possibly military characteristics of the site. There is, in fact, only one find of a specifically military nature from the site (harness stud <S26>). Equally, little in the form of the monument bears out the original interpretation and alternative functions for this element of the site must, therefore, be considered.

Although the structure was evidently of a respectable size in plan (*c* 5m^2 internally) and may, consequently, have been correspondingly tall, we have no evidence for height as the structure had been demolished to ground level. The foundations, subsequently largely robbed, were only 450mm deep which is surprisingly shallow in view of the near 2.0m thickness of the walls, indicating perhaps that the structure may have been only one storey tall.

Stone-built signal towers are rare in Britain; turf and timber structures are, for a number of reasons, much more commonly encountered. Masonry signal stations are known from Holyhead Mountain (Crew 1982) and the East Yorkshire coast.

The Yorkshire coast examples from Huntcliff, Goldsborough, Scarborough and Filey exhibit a common plan, consisting of a central tower surrounded by a curtain wall and ditch (Ottaway 1995). The central towers are more substantial than the Shadwell example, varying in breadth from 12.0m to 15.0m (Ottaway 1995; von Petrikovits 1971, 197–99; Hornsby and Stanton 1912) compared to 9.0m at Shadwell. The walls of the towers are even more substantial than those at Shadwell being up to 2.5m thick, compared to 1.90m. In some cases additional support seems to have been provided by piers or columns. The slighter nature of the structure and the absence of characteristic features, such as encircling ditches, upcast bank or curtain wall, argue against a military interpretation of the Shadwell 'tower'.

A signal station, like any other Roman military installation, would have formed part of a defensive system. However, it is difficult to identify any other elements of such a system which might be associated with a putative 'tower' at Shadwell. In nearly three decades since the Shadwell structure was discovered no comparable military sites have come to light in the Thames estuary or London area. Although the construction of the 'tower' cannot be precisely dated it is probable that it was built before the mid 3rd century. This predates the earliest coastal defences at Burgh Castle and Richborough (von Petrikovits 1971) and considerably predates the Yorkshire coast stations which are now thought to date from the last decades of the 4th century (Ottaway 1995), although it may be similar in date to the fort at Reculver (Detsicas 1983, 24 n 30).

If the interpretation of the masonry structure as a signal tower is untenable, then alternative interpretations should be sought. One possibility is that it represents the cella of a temple or shrine. From the general form of the structure, this is not impossible and its situation on a slight eminence, making it a prominent feature when viewed from the river, is perhaps not dissimilar to the position of the probable temple in Greenwich Park (Sheldon and Yule 1979). The apparent absence of an ambulatory might be explained away, either by extensive post-Roman truncation or by a failure of the excavator to spot more insubstantial, possibly timber, remains of the ambulatory, both rather unlikely. The large quantity of coins from the sites might, superficially, suggest a religious aspect to the finds assemblage (the difficulties of interpreting coin evidence are discussed in Chapter 5.6). More striking, however, is the complete absence of the votive objects and statuettes which are the most characteristic features of finds assemblages of religious sites and comparison with the Greenwich material is most telling on this point.

A more tenable interpretation would have the structure as a mausoleum. There are a number of points in favour of this. The first is the form of the structure: a number of free-standing square structures have been encountered in London and the adjacent counties which have been interpreted as mausolea (for example, Detsicas 1983; Barber and Bowsher 2000; Mackinder 2000; Fletcher and Meates 1969; Farwell and Molleson 1993); some have even been thought to be tower-like in appearance.

Examples of mausolea in London have been found in the eastern cemetery and at Southwark. Seven masonry structures were noted in recent excavations at the eastern cemetery (Barber and Bowsher 2000, 111–14). Although all of the structures were only partly seen or fragmentary, it was possible to reconstruct their overall dimensions in most cases. The largest was 3.5m by 5.8m in size with foundations 0.75m wide; the remainder varied between 2.4m and 3.2m in breadth and between 2.6m and 4.0m in length. Recent excavations at Great Dover Street in Southwark have uncovered two masonry structures which have been interpreted as possible mausolea. One structure was thought to be a temple/mausoleum set within a walled precinct. The *cella* of the temple/mausoleum was 4.7m long and 4.2m wide and was set within a precinct approximately 8.0m square (Mackinder 2000, 8–10). The second structure was interpreted as a possible mausoleum and was roughly 6.0m square with shallow buttresses on its north and south faces (Mackinder 2000, 16–18). The walls of both structures were approximately 0.80m thick.

A rapid survey of mausolea from elsewhere in the country indicates that the London examples are not untypical in their dimensions and construction. The probable mausoleum at Stone by Faversham, Kent, was 5.3m long and 4.8m wide with foundations 1.2m to 2.0m thick (Fletcher and Meates 1969). At Poundbury, Dorset, two of the nine mausolea exceeded 6.0m in size; the remainder lay in the range 3.9m to 5.0m. Where noted, the thickness of the foundations did not exceed 1.0m (Farwell and Molleson 1993, 45).

Although towards the larger end of the range of such structures, the Shadwell 'tower' is not dissimilar in appearance to the 'tower' mausoleum from Langley in Kent (Jessup 1959, 26–7) and has buttresses similar to those noted at Southwark and on one of the mausolea at Lullingstone. Unfortunately, the almost complete lack of evidence regarding the interior of the Shadwell structure does not help the comparison. A strong point in favour of the interpretation as a mausoleum is the evident use of the Shadwell site for burials, most particularly the apparent inhumation noted inside the structure. That this is not a decisive point in the interpretation of the structure is a result of the limited nature of the records from the LD74 excavation. The burial is poorly described and may even post-date the use of the 'tower'; if it could be shown to be a contemporary feature it would be compelling, but new evidence is unlikely to materialise. A possibly significant hint of the funerary nature of the structure is perhaps provided by the nature of the accessioned finds assemblage noted below.

The dating of this structure is almost as problematic as determining its function. The absence of appropriate plan or section evidence means that its precise position within the sequence cannot be determined. There are, however, a number of pointers, the best of which relate to the disuse and destruction of the structure. It was out of use by, and robbed following, the industrial activity of period 4 and may well have been disused, although still standing, when that activity started. That is to say, its initial function no longer continued after the 330s/340s. Its construction date is more difficult to estimate. All other Roman features seem to respect its position and there are no features apparently predating it. As a consequence, therefore, it is possible that the structure is amongst the earliest features on the site. It is tempting to place the building in the period of maximum activity on the site, that is the late 3rd century (if the quantity of material of this date is a genuine indicator of maximum activity). This would, however, be difficult to accommodate with an interpretation of the feature as a mausoleum, period 3 being notably lacking in burials. It is possible to view the structure as providing a focus for the burials of period 2 in which case it would have had a long lifespan (potentially from *c* AD 100 to *c* AD 360). In view of the signs of structural collapse noted in the few surviving remains of the building, it might well be that it soon ceased to be used for burials, gradually crumbling away until finally demolished in the later 4th century.

The bulk of the finds including the samian, other pottery, glass and animal bone were recovered from the period 3 ditches. The pottery exhibited signs of use but little abrasion and included a high incidence of sherd links, as did some of the glass, suggesting the material was derived from nearby. The nature of any adjacent or nearby settlement is not clear from these assemblages.

The supposed military character of the Shadwell sites is not wholly supported by the artefactual assemblage. One mount is in fact of military type, a vulvate stud with hanger from horse harness (<S26>, Fig 25), but its context is uncertain. Such mounts, which date from the 3rd century, are comparatively rare in London, but other examples have been found in the city where the presence of soldiers at all periods cannot be doubted. The other mounts come from the Cheapside/Walbrook area (Hill and Woodger 1999, 54) and north-west Southwark (Wardle in prep), the latter a domestic/industrial area. In fact,

Fig 13 Ceramic lamps <S22> *(length* 101.5mm) *and* <S21> *(length* 90.5mm)

the proportion of military artefacts recovered at Shadwell is actually smaller (one in 700) than in some other parts of London and one mount cannot be used as *prima facie* evidence of a military function for the building. However, the date and composition of the samian group from Shadwell has close parallels in contemporary sites with a military connection and may suggest some kind of military presence in the vicinity of the site (see Chapter 5.2).

The small finds are atypical for an urban assemblage. Disregarding the very large number of coins, the group as a whole consists of glassware and items of a personal nature such as hairpins and jewellery, the latter in no great quantity. There are very few domestic utensils, although two complete *firmalampen* (Fig 13) came from a late group. Many of the types of identified finds are more often seen in funerary contexts. The same may be said of certain glass vessels particularly those which were intact, or nearly so, when deposited. Jewellery and dress accessories are frequently seen as grave goods and most of the complete lamps found in London have come from grave deposits. Unfortunately, it has not been possible to ascribe any of these objects from Shadwell to specific funerary contexts. Most are from open areas, ditches and gullies and are certainly redeposited, either from earlier structures or perhaps from disturbed graves. Interpretation of the later Roman jewellery, the shale bracelets or the jet hairpin, as displaced grave goods would further imply that a cemetery continued to exist into the late 3rd/4th century, corresponding to the excavated evidence for inhumation burials in period 5.

Uncertainty about the eastern limit of Roman London's eastern cemetery must, in view of the relative proximity of the study area to the easternmost known burials, lead to careful consideration of the origin of burial in the study area. The presence here of nine cremation burials, all dated to the first half of the 2nd century, does not amount to the same long-term and intensive burial practice seen in the burial zone closer to the city. Nonetheless, a similarity in date between the earliest burials in both areas and the earlier use of the burial areas for gravel extraction, a practice noted widely in the eastern cemetery, might suggest that the Shadwell sites lay in an area initially intended for burials, which was at first treated in the same way as the zone closer to the urban area but was subsequently deemed to be surplus to requirements.

Alternatively it is possible, by analogy with similar features at Old Ford, to see the burials at Shadwell as indicative of the presence nearby of a settlement. Variation in use of the area between burials and other agricultural or industrial functions might more closely parallel the development of a small hinterland settlement, where burials were less closely regulated than in more major urban agglomerations. The period 3 animal bone assemblage exhibits urban, rural and industrial traits. The use of a cleaver is characteristic of urban rather than rural butchery. As well as evidence for locally reared cattle, sheep/goat and goat, the assemblage also suggests the post-mortem use of animal parts for industrial purposes.

4

Conclusions

From the chronological survey, it is clear that the Roman period at Shadwell saw multi-phase, multi-function development of the site over a much greater time span than has hitherto been suspected. At first sight it would appear that changes on the site occurred by fits and starts and were followed by substantial periods of time with little or no change. The first period of activity seems to lie in the late 1st or early 2nd century and included quarrying and subsequent reuse of the site for cremation burials (S1, the 'tower', may have formed a focus for these burials). The next activity occurred in the later 3rd century when landscape division was undertaken, with the construction of fence lines, subsequently replaced by ditches and gullies. The rectilinear timber building (B1), perhaps a shed or barn, was constructed at the same time. The associated animal bone evidence suggests that butchery may have taken place on or near the site, perhaps indicating that the site lay near a droving route supplying the city of Londinium, just over a kilometre away, or a nearby settlement.

A rather shorter hiatus seems then to have been followed in the middle decades of the 4th century by the establishment of what appears to have been an industrial complex. This industrial use of the site seems to have ceased in the later 4th century and was followed by the final demolition of the 'tower' and the possible reuse of the site for burials.

At least four distinct types of activity seem to be represented successively on the site, in three chronologically distinct periods. The sequence of burial use, followed by apparent settlement, craft or industrial use and finally a return to burial use is perhaps both more diverse and longer than is usual for a hinterland site. Other facets of Roman Shadwell are also indicative of the unusual nature of the area: the pottery and coin assemblages are, for example unusually large for a non-urban site and exhibit a number of peculiarities. While these peculiarities are discussed in Chapter 5, the caveats regarding interpretation of finds evidence, laid out in the coin report, should be emphasised here, with the additional note that the nature of the stratigraphic record from the Shadwell sites does not allow the fine teasing-out of detail which would be possible on more recently excavated sites. Straight comparison of quantities may be misleading: for example, the small quantities of 1st- and 2nd-century coins from the site may represent a more significant loss rate than the relatively much greater quantities of 3rd- and 4th-century coins. Equally, the examination of comparative assemblages should perhaps be treated with caution: in the absence of definitive evidence for military presence on or near the site, is it possible to establish the reasons why the samian assemblage bears comparison with contemporary assemblages from military sites? The animal bone assemblage seems to show butchery in more than domestic quantity, similarly indicating a degree of activity unmatched by the structural remains.

The quantity of bone, pottery and metallic finds from the site is out of proportion to the structural remains seen and, whilst some of the finds are clearly or probably funerary in character, the remainder are domestic. There would seem, therefore, to be a case for suggesting the presence very near by of a large or high status farm or settlement. Further comparison with other hinterland settlements such as Old Ford, Staines and Enfield may prove fruitful.

Although the problems inherent in assigning dates to the successive periods of activity have been highlighted above, and have by no means been resolved, it is nonetheless apparent that Roman Shadwell has an unusual chronological profile. All categories of datable material show a distinct peak in the second half of the 3rd-century. If this genuinely represents the period of maximum activity, then it is in striking contrast to the currently-perceived cycle, of 2nd-century boom followed by 3rd-century depression and 4th-century revival, posited for Londinium and its hinterland.

Roman Shadwell is clearly unusual: it is possible to say how; it is unfortunately not possible to say why.

5

Specialist appendices

5.1 Roman (non-samian) pottery

Fiona Seeley

Methodology

Previous work

The majority of the non-samian pottery from LD76 was identified, spot dated and quantified by EVEs and weight by Beth Richardson in the early 1980s. The non-samian pottery from LD74 was not available at the time of study, although some pieces had been published in earlier corpora (Young 1977; Lyne and Jeffries 1979). Fabrics were given common-name codes and fabric numbers. The type series established by Marsh and Tyers (1979) was used to record the pottery forms. However, because this typology concentrates mainly on pottery from the early Roman period (up to the mid 2nd century), late forms were only recorded by their basic type such as jar, bowl, dish. For example, the quantified data do not, therefore, show the true proportions between bag-shaped (3J), necked globular (3K) and pentice (3L) beakers, for only where a reference was given in the original records to a publication has the beaker been identified as a specific form. The basic types were supplemented by a 'corpus number' which referred to an illustrated example of that type of vessel (DUA 1984). No full report has been located for this work.

Subsequent work

All stratified pottery data were checked with the corresponding material to see if the database was complete and correct with the existing archive The non-samian pottery identifications and the weight and EVEs were not re-examined so remain as originally recorded. The plain and decorated samian was quantified by weight and EVEs. Since the mid 1980s the list of MoLAS fabric and form codes, especially for the late Roman period, has been extended and altered; therefore all codes were updated. Where possible, corpus numbers were used to identify specific forms. All fabric identifications are those given originally except for the Campanian black sand Dressel 2–4 fabric (CAMP1) and the diagnostically early fabric, Sugar Loaf Court ware (SLOW). These have been changed as their original identifications were not correct.

Full expansions of the pottery codes used are in Davies et al (1994) for the early period and Symonds and Tomber (1991) for the later period (see above Tables 2–4). Amphora fabrics which have been identified across the site but not sourced are differentiated by a numeral after the term AMPH, for example AMPH1, AMPH2. No further work was possible within the scope of the project to analyse the unsourced amphora fabrics, but given the dominance of 3rd-century pottery on the site, it is probable that they are late Roman in date.

The non-samian pottery reported on in this publication is from assemblages securely assigned to Roman contexts. However, all decorated samian from both Roman and post-Roman deposits has been catalogued (Chapter 5.2). This difference in treatment is a result of the historical development of the project.

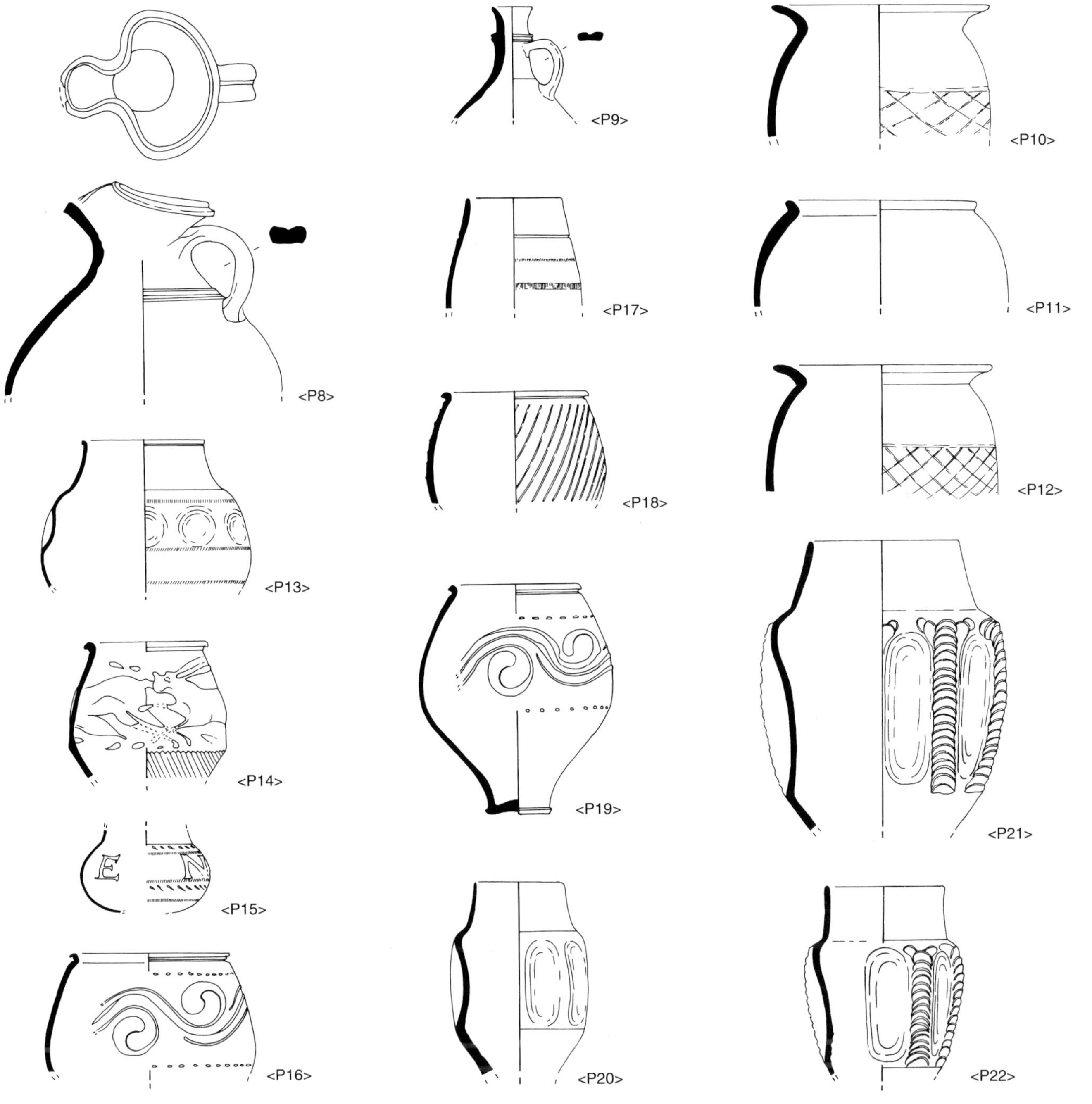

Fig 14 Roman pottery flagons <P8>–<P9>, jars <P10>–<P12> and beakers < P13>–<P22> (scale 1:4)

Results

The pottery assemblage from LD76 is defined by three main phases. The first is dated to the late 1st–early 2nd century and it consists of mostly complete vessels which have been used as cremation vessels. The second main phase is dated to the middle two quarters of the 3rd century and the majority of the pottery, including material that is from later contexts or is unphased or unstratified, can be dated to this period. The largest stratified assemblage from this phase (the boundary ditch, S4) is discussed in Chapter 2.3 (and see Figs 14,15). The third phase is dated to the mid–late 4th century. The most notable pottery assemblages are discussed by land use and, where substantial assemblages occur, these are supported by tables of quantification by fabric or form (Tables 5–10). The pottery and full paper archive have been deposited in the LAARC.

5.2 Samian wares

Joanna Bird

Introduction

The samian is of particular interest for its date – it includes some of the latest samian from Britain – and for the high proportion of late East Gaulish wares present. For a relatively small assemblage, the samian comes from a wide range of sources, probably reflecting the proximity of the site to London. In addition to Gaulish wares, there is a decorated bowl by 'potter A' of Colchester, whose products are rare outside the immediate vicinity of Colchester itself, and a single sherd from an African red slip ware platter of 3rd-

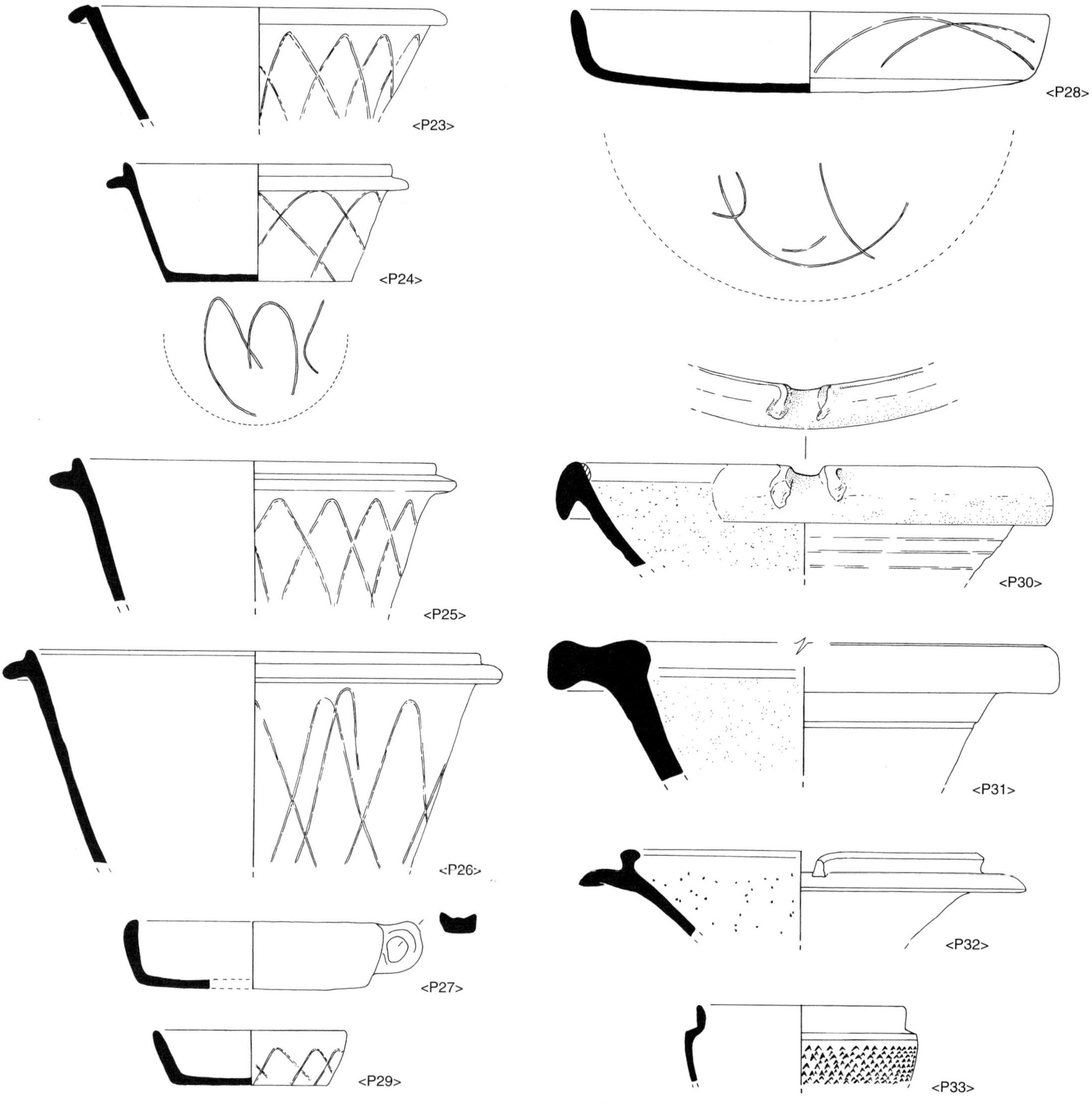

Fig 15 Roman pottery bowls <P23>–<P26>, dishes <P27>–<P29>, mortaria <P30>–<P32> and box <P33> (scale 1:4)

or early 4th-century date. The samian is generally in poor condition, but very little is too damaged to be identified. On a simple sherd count, the percentages of samian from the main source areas are: South Gaul 6%, Central Gaul 27%, East Gaul 67%. The sources of the decorated samian are shown on Table 11, the identified forms from each production area on Table 12. There is a concordance table for the catalogued decorated samian, in catalogue number order and by source, in broadly chronological order except for <SAM 75>–<SAM79> (Table 13).

The South Gaulish wares comprise five unattributed decorated bowls from La Graufesenque, dating from the Neronian period to the Trajanic, and a bowl by Chresimus or an associated potter at Montans, of Hadrianic to early Antonine date. A bowl of late Flavian to Trajanic date is interesting for its clumsy finishing, and would appear to be a 'second' (<SAM5>, Fig 17). There are no definitely pre-Flavian plain forms present, and only one example of Drag 15/17; nor are there any South Gaulish stamps. This scarcity of South Gaulish samian, together with the evidence from the Central Gaulish wares, indicates a very low level of occupation on the site before the Hadrianic period at the earliest.

Central Gaulish ware from Les Martres-de-Veyre consists of a single decorated bowl by the Hadrianic to early Antonine potter Cettus, and some five plain-ware sherds of Drag 18/31,

Table 11 The sources of the decorated samian

Kiln-site	No. of bowls	%
South Gaul		
La Graufesenque	5	7
Montans	1	>1
Central Gaul		
Les Martres-de-Veyre	1	>1
Lezoux	13	18
East Gaul		
La Madeleine	1	>1
Lavoye	1	>1
Trier	13	18
Rheinzabern	37	51
Britain		
Colchester	1	>1
Total	**73**	

Drag 27 and Déch 67. None of the Trajanic makers of decorated ware is represented. The Lezoux ware is largely Antonine, and the decorated bowls include one each by the Sacer-Attianus group and Pugnus, between two and four by the Cinnamus group, one or two by Paternus II and between two and four by the Doeccus-Casurius group. The identified plain-ware stamps, of Paullus v and Severianus i, are of mid to later Antonine date, but the later Antonine plain forms are relatively uncommon: six sherds of mortaria, four of Walters 79/Ludowici Tg, and six of Drag 31R.

Apart from single sherds of decorated bowls from La Madeleine, in the style associated with Ricken's ovolo Cb, and from Lavoye, probably by Gesatus, the East Gaulish wares come from Trier and Rheinzabern. There are 13 decorated bowls from Trier, including single bowls of Werkstatt I, Werkstatt I or II and Dexter, and two each by Criciro, Afer, Dubitatus-Dubitus and the Primanus group. The latest potter here is Primanus, who is dated *c* AD 235–50. While the actual mould-makers range in date from the Hadrianic/early Antonine period to the middle of the 3rd century, there is evidence from Trier that potters of the mid 3rd century sometimes used the moulds of earlier mould-makers (Huld-Zetsche 1972, 81–8). This is certainly likely to be the case with <SAM27> (Fig 18), by Criciro, which is made from a worn mould and has the massive footring characteristic of bowls made after *c* AD 230 (Bird 1993, 4; Huld-Zetsche 1998, 148); a similar footring is present on <SAM32> by Dubitatus-Dubitus, who was active *c* AD 225–45 (Fig 18). Equally, some of the bowls are in the very pale yellowish or pink fabrics characteristic of the mid 3rd century 'Massenfund' group at Trier (Huld-Zetsche 1971, 22) and found in the St Magnus House group of *c* AD 235–45 (Bird 1986, 143): they include <SAM23>, by Werkstatt I Stufe A, <SAM30>, by Afer, <SAM31>, and <SAM35>, by the Primanus group (Fig 18). While the remaining sherds are individually less diagnostic, it is likely that much if not all of the decorated Trier ware dates from around the second quarter of the 3rd century.

Table 12 The identified samian forms from each main production area, based on a sherd count, showing the maximum possible number of vessels

Form	South Gaul	Central Gaul	East Gaul
Drag 15/17	1		
Drag 15/17 or 18	1		
Drag 18	10		
Drag 18R	1		
Drag 18/31	1	9	1
Drag 18/31 or 31		1	3
Drag 27	4	2	
Drag 27 or 35	1		
Drag 29	5		
Drag 30		5	3
Drag 30 or 37		6	17
Drag 30 or Déch 68		1	
Drag 31		13	
Drag 31/Lud Sa			27
Drag 31 or 31R		3	
Drag 31R		6	
Drag 31R/Lud Sb			19
Drag 31/33 variant			1
Drag 31/37R variant			3
Drag 32			28
Drag 33		26	17
Drag 36			2
Drag 37	1	28	93
Drag 38		3	19
Drag 41			3
Drag 43 or 45 (mortarium)		2	21
Drag 45		1	19
Déch 67		1	
Déch 68 or 72		2	
Knorr 78	1		
Wa 79		2	
Wa 79 or Lud Tg		1	
Wa 79R or Lud TgR		1	
Wa 81		1	
Cu 15		1	
Cu 21		2	1
Cu 21 or mortarium		1	1
Lud SMb/c			1
Lud Tk			2
Indented beaker probably cf Ludowici Va			1
Beaker/jar, Lud V series			4
Closed form			6
Bowl			2
Dish			3
Totals: no. (%)	**26 (6%)**	**118 (27%)**	**297 (67%)**

Rheinzabern products make up 51% of all the decorated ware, a proportion so far unique in Britain; the mould-makers represented range in date from the Antonine period to the middle of the 3rd century. After the early 3rd century it becomes more difficult to assign close dates to individual Rheinzabern mould-makers, and the problem of dating is compounded by evidence from the kiln-site indicating that, as at Trier, earlier moulds were sometimes reused by potters active towards the middle of the 3rd century (Reutti 1983, 54–60; Bittner 1986, 254–55). This is certainly likely to be the case with <SAM39> (Fig 19), in the style of 'Kreis des Cerialis ware B', which has a disproportionately high flaring rim, a characteristic of late bowls (Bird 1993, 4); the stamped Comitialis V bowl <SAM41> is probably also later, to judge from its fabric and finish (Fig 19). While there are a few pieces which may date from the Antonine period to the early 3rd century, it is probable that, as with the Trier wares, the majority of the decorated Rheinzabern bowls are to be dated well within the 3rd century, a date which would fit with the evidence currently available for the majority of the mould-makers represented (<SAM43>–<SAM67>, Figs 19–21).

Research in recent years has concentrated on establishing a relative chronology for the Rheinzabern mould-makers, using a variety of statistical techniques to define which workshops were working simultaneously or successively, sharing or passing on individual motif and figure punches, and examining which styles occur together in those assemblages for which some dating evidence is available (Simon 1968; Bernhard 1981; Bittner 1986 and 1996; Mees 1993; Kortüm and Mees 1998). In all these studies, the most numerous potters at Shadwell – Julius II–Julianus I (five bowls), Primitivus I and IV (six or seven) and the Julius I–Lupus group (two or three) – are found towards the end of the sequence, while a small number of recent excavations have provided more definite dating evidence. A kiln stokehole at Rheinzabern (Grube 17c, Rhz. 79/657) contained the wasters from a failed firing, including 92 bowls of Julius II–Julianus I, 77 of Primitivus I and 37 of Julius I–Lupus; it is dated *c* AD 235–45 (Reutti 1983, 54–7; Bittner 1986, 249–52). The second 'shipment' group at St Magnus House, also dated *c* AD 235–45, included 19 bowls of the Julius II group, two of Primitivus I and IV and 12 of Julius I–Lupus, associated with bowls of the late Trier potters Dubitatus–Dubitus (at least four) and the Primanus group (four) (Bird 1986, figs 81, 83). A group of samian found in Keller 1 at Langenhain came from the collapse of a burnt store overhead; it is dated *c* AD 233 or a little later, and included bowls of Julius I–Lupus (at least 19) associated with bowls of Dubitatus–Dubitus (at least 45) (Simon and Köhler 1992, 86–97).

According to the dating indicated by Simon (1968) and Bernhard (1981), the latest Rheinzabern potters present at Shadwell are Victor I, Perpetuus and Pervincus I, and this, with the evidence discussed above for both Trier and Rheinzabern, would indicate a date *c* AD 225–50 for much of the Shadwell samian assemblage (although these three potters are absent from the St Magnus House group, there are single bowls of Pervincus and Perpetuus from what is probably part of the same deposit at Billingsgate: Brigham (1990), table 6, phases II.2 and III.1). This dating is also suggested by the heavy late footrings of <SAM49> by Helenius, and <SAM58> (Fig 20), stamped by Julius II, and by the high rim-bands of <SAM39> (Fig 19), in the style of 'Kreis des Cerialis ware B', <SAM48> by Verecundus II, <SAM55> and <SAM57>, by Primitivus IV (Fig 20), <SAM59> by Julius II–Julianus I, and <SAM65> by Perpetuus (Fig 21). The identified plain-ware stamps, of Pateriva of Trier and of Maianus iii and Peppo of Rheinzabern, though not themselves closely datable, could also fit into this date range. In addition to the more common forms such as Lud Sa and Sb (Drag 31 series), Drag 32 and mortaria, the plain wares from both kiln-sites include uncommon forms, some of which are likely to be late: incised cups of form Drag 41 (<SAM75>–<SAM77>, Fig 21), a rouletted variant of Drag 31/37 (Bird 1993, fig 3), the barbotine bowl Lud SMb/c, the dish Lud Tk, and several beakers and small jars, perhaps including Lud Va.

What explanation can be offered for the presence of a samian assemblage of this date and composition on an extra-mural site such as Shadwell? While the proximity of London would explain the wide range of sources for the pottery, it does not account for the high proportion of late Trier and Rheinzabern wares, as a comparison between the distribution by date of the Shadwell decorated ware and that from London clearly shows (Fig 16). Apart from London, Colchester seems to have the largest overall quantity of Trier and Rheinzabern samian in Britain. As an interesting comparison with Shadwell, the catalogue of decorated samian from several recent major excavations there includes only 39 Trier bowls (3% of the total) and 81 Rheinzabern (6.3%), some of which are clearly of 2nd-century date, from a total of 1288 (Bird 1999, nos 1164–1283).

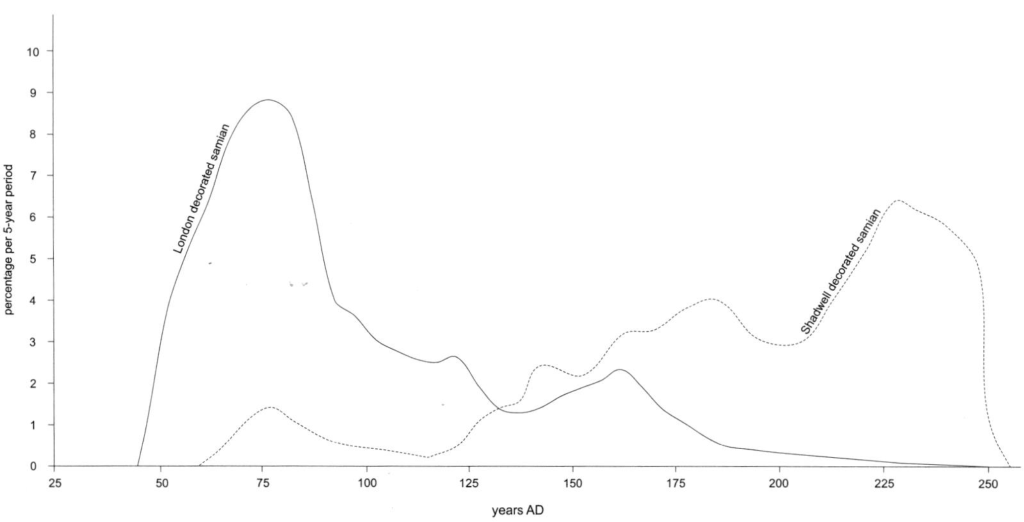

Fig 16 The distribution by date of the decorated samian from Shadwell compared with London as a whole (London distribution after Marsh 1981)

Marsh (1981) has demonstrated that the London pattern is characteristic of British sites with continuous occupation during the Roman period; the divergence from it at Shadwell must, therefore, be due to the circumstances and chronology of the site. There is so far only one site in Britain with a comparable assemblage of late East Gaulish wares, the Roman quay at St Magnus House, London (Bird 1986); there they apparently belonged to a single shipment of *c* AD 235–45, and could be explained by the special, commercial, nature of the site.

Such an explanation is unlikely for the late Shadwell samian: even where there are cross-joins, the bowls are generally too incomplete to suggest that they come directly from a shop or warehouse. On the other hand, the rarity of such an assemblage in Britain does imply that the majority of the late samian ware reached the site at approximately the same time, in response to a specific demand. Unfortunately, the stratigraphic record provides little help, with most of the samian from Roman contexts coming from ditch fills and areas of pitting. The largest group, including ten decorated Rheinzabern bowls and the rouletted Drag 31/37 variant, came from the fill of the phase 6 ditch (S4), which also contained a very large assemblage of other pottery probably dating to the third quarter of the 3rd century.

Since the Shadwell site does not lie within a major town, some kind of military presence in the vicinity of the site around the second quarter of the 3rd century might provide an explanation. The 3rd-century fort at Piercebridge, for example, has a small amount of late samian, including a bowl of the Trier Primanus group (Ward 1993, 18–19; M Ward, pers comm), while the 3rd-century fortified site at Caister-on-Sea, with an overall ratio of Central to East Gaulish wares of 1:3, has decorated bowls of Dubitatus–Dubitus of Trier and the late Rheinzabern potter Severianus, as well as late plain flagons (Dickinson 1993). Mees has commented that the Rheinzabern decorated assemblage at Shadwell fits well with groups from military sites in Germania Inferior and northern Germania Superior; on his graph (1994, fig 9) Shadwell fits into the lower right quadrant, aligning horizontally with Holzhausen and vertically a little to the left of Dormagen (A Mees, pers comm). However, since the structural and stratigraphic evidence is insufficient to support Johnson's interpretation of the building as a signal-station, the problem posed by the late samian ware at Shadwell must remain unresolved.

Catalogue of decorated and plain samian

The catalogue is ordered by phase, land use and context (see Chapter 1.3–1.4); a concordance table is given which orders the catalogued decorated samian, in catalogue number order and by source in broadly chronological order, except for <SAM75>–<SAM79> (Table 13). Where a decorated samian vessel is present in more than one land use, the full catalogue details are given under its earliest stratigraphic appearance on site and subsequent entries refer back to this first entry, which can be found from Table 13. The plain samian which is unstratified or from unphased contexts is not listed in this catalogue. Separate catalogues of the decorated wares (ordered by pottery of origin) and all of the plain wares (ordered by feature/context number) are held in the archive. The following abbreviations have been used.

Dragendorff (Drag)
Déchelette (Déch)
Curle (Cu)
Ludowici (Lud)
Walters (Wa)
South Gaulish (SG)
Central Gaulish (CG)
East Gaulish (EG)
Ludowici and Ricken 1948 (*LR*)
Figure and motif types from Ricken and Fischer 1963 (*RF*)
Stanfield and Simpson 1958 (*SS*)
Figure types from Oswald 1936–7 (*Oswald*)

Items in the samian catalogue are cross-referenced to the potters' stamps catalogue.

Phase 2 Open Area 2

LD76 [306]
Drag 37, EG, late 2nd–mid 3rd century.

LD76 [307]
<SAM59>, Fig 21, (also LD76 [255] [645] [648] [710] [732]) Drag 37. Rheinzabern. In the style of Julius II–Julianus I, who are recorded for all the motifs: ovolo *RF*.E23, cross O53 and medallions K7 and K14. Cf *LR* Taf 204 for a group of similar bowls. *c* AD 225–50. The band between rim and decoration is 55mm high.

LD76 [629]
<SAM64>, Fig 21, (also LD76 [663] [736], unphased, LD76 [281], LD74 [F29]) Drag 37. Rheinzabern. In the style of Victor I, the only recorded user of the ovolo, *RF*.E6; he also used the cockerel T239a, rosette O34a and medallion K19a. Cf *LR* Taf 232, nos 4, 9. Second quarter 3rd century, probably. The band between rim and decoration is 40mm high.
Drag 45, EG, late 2nd–mid 3rd century.

LD76 [663]
<SAM64> see LD76 [629] Drag 37. Rheinzabern.
Drag 31, CG, Antonine.

LD76 [710]
<SAM1>, Fig 17, (also LD76 [645]) Drag 29. La Graufesenque. Upper zone scroll with spurred buds and spiral tendrils, and rosettes in the field. *c* AD 65–85.
<SAM40>, Fig 19, Drag 37. Rheinzabern. With mould-stamp of Secundinus–Avitus (<STAMP7>, Fig 23), associated with the style of Comitialis I. The scroll decoration composed of the beaded festoon *RF*.KB95 is shown on a bowl with this stamp on *LR* Taf 79, no. 12; the scroll, leaf P42 and what may be the same figure (a gladiator, M225) are on Taf 79, no. 13. *c* AD 175–220.
<SAM44>, Fig 19, Drag 37. Rheinzabern. The ovolo, *RF*.E42, was shared by Julius I, Lupus and Perpetuus; the motif beneath is not identifiable. First half 3rd century. The band between rim and decoration is 35mm high.
<SAM59> see LD76 [307] Drag 37. Rheinzabern.
Drag 37?, EG, later 2nd–mid 3rd century. EG sherd.

Table 13 Concordance table of the catalogued decorated samian in catalogue number order and by source in broadly chronological order

Catalogue no.	Form	Site	Phase	Land use	Context	Comments
La Graufesenque, Fig 17						
<SAM1>	Drag 29	LD76	2	OA2	[710]	
<SAM2>	Drag 29	LD76	6	S4	[360]	
<SAM3>	Drag 37	LD76	2	OA2	[1305]	
<SAM4>	Knorr 78	LD74	8	OA9	[197]	
<SAM5>	Drag 37	LD76	6	S4	[361]	
Montans, Fig 17						
<SAM6>	Drag 37	LD74	unphased		[251.1]	
Les Martres-de-Veyre, Fig 17						
<SAM7>	Drag 37	LD74	unphased		[F17A]	
Lezoux, Fig 17						
<SAM8>	Drag 37	LD74	unphased		[F17C]	
<SAM9>	Drag 37	LD74	unphased		[251.1]	
<SAM10>	Drag 37	LD76	2	OA2	[736]	
<SAM11>	Drag 37	LD74	unphased		[F17A]	
<SAM12>	Drag 37	LD74	6	OA7	[303]	
<SAM13>	Drag 30	LD76	6	S4	[278]	
<SAM14>	Drag 30 or Déch 68	LD74	unphased		[F31]	
<SAM15>	Drag 37	LD74	unphased		[251.1]	
<SAM16>	Drag 37	LD74	unphased		[F17A]	
<SAM17>	Drag 37	LD76	unphased		[734]	
<SAM18>	Drag 37	LD74	unphased		[74.1]	
<SAM19>	Drag 37	LD74	8	OA9	[4.3]	
<SAM20>	Drag 37	LD74	9	OA10	[2]	
La Madeleine, Fig 18						
<SAM21>	Drag 37	LD74	unphased		[22.2]	
Lavoye, Fig 18						
<SAM22>	Drag 37	LD76	6	S4	[261]	
Trier, Fig 18						
<SAM23>	Drag 37	LD74	9	OA10	[114]	
<SAM24>	Drag 37	LD74	unphased		[4.3]	
<SAM25>	Drag 37	LD74	unphased		[4.4]	
<SAM26>	Drag 37	LD76	6	B1	[301]	
<SAM27>	Drag 37	LD76	7	S8	[18]	
<SAM28>	Drag 37	LD74	unphased		[289]	
<SAM29>	Drag 37	LD74	7	S8	[18]	
<SAM30>	Drag 37	LD74	9	OA10	[114]	
<SAM31>	Drag 37	LD74	unphased		[251.1]	
<SAM32>	Drag 37	LD74	unphased		[289]	
<SAM33>	Drag 37	LD74	8	OA9	[197]	
<SAM34>	Drag 37	LD74	unphased		[186]	
<SAM35>	Drag 37	LD74	9	OA10	[114]	
Rheinzabern, Figs 19–21						
<SAM36>	Drag 30	LD74	unphased		[289.1]	
<SAM37>	Drag 37	LD74	7	S9	[19]	
<SAM38>	Drag 37	LD74	9	OA10	[2]	
<SAM39>	Drag 37	LD74	unphased		[F21]	
<SAM40>	Drag 37	LD76	2	OA2	[710]	<STAMP7>, Fig 22
<SAM41>	Drag 37	LD74	7	S8	[18]	<STAMP1>, Fig 22
<SAM42>	Drag 37	LD74	7	S8	[18]	
<SAM43>	Drag 37	LD76	6	S4	[360]	
<SAM44>	Drag 37	LD76	2	OA2	[710]	
<SAM45>	Drag 37	LD74	unphased		[251.1]	
<SAM46>	Drag 37	LD76	7	S8	[240]	
<SAM47>	Drag 37	LD76	6	S4	[261]	
<SAM48>	Drag 37	LD74	unphased		[251.1]	
<SAM49>	Drag 37	LD74	7	S8	[18]	
<SAM50>	Drag 37	LD76	6	S4	[370]	
<SAM51>	Drag 37	LD74	unphased		[171.1]	

(*Table 13 cont*)

Catalogue no.	Form	Site	Phase	Land use	Context	Comments
<SAM52>	Drag 37	LD76	6	S4	[261]	
<SAM53>	Drag 30	LD74	9	OA10	[4.1]	
<SAM54>	Drag 37	LD74	unphased		[F29]	
<SAM55>	Drag 37	LD76	6	S4	[361]	
<SAM56>	Drag 37	LD76	6	S4	[261]	
<SAM57>	Drag 37	LD76	6	S4	[261]	
<SAM58>	Drag 37	LD76	6	B1	[700]	<STAMP2>, Fig 22
<SAM59>	Drag 37	LD76	2	OA2	[307]	
<SAM60>	Drag 37	LD76	7	OA8	[255]	
<SAM61>	Drag 37	LD74	8	OA9	[233.2]	
<SAM62>	Drag 37	LD76	6	S4	[651]	
<SAM63>	Drag 37	LD74	unphased		[289]	
<SAM64>	Drag 37	LD76	2	OA2	[629]	
<SAM65>	Drag 37	LD76	6	S4	[261]	
<SAM66>	Drag 37	LD74	unphased		[189]	
<SAM67>	Drag 37	LD74	8	OA9	[197]	
<SAM68>	Drag 37	LD74	unphased		[251.1]	
<SAM69>	Drag 37	LD74	unphased		[F6]	
<SAM71>	Drag 37	LD76	6	S4	[659]	
<SAM72>	Drag 37	LD74	9	OA10	[114]	
Colchester, Fig 21						
<SAM73>	Drag 37	LD74	unphased		[F17A]	
Central Gaul, Fig 21						
<SAM74>	large jar or beaker	LD76	10	OA11	[285]	appliqué
Rheinzabern, <SAM75>–<SAM76> Fig 21						
<SAM75>	Drag 41	LD74	7	S8	[18]	incised
<SAM76>	Drag 41	LD76	unphased		[137]	incised
<SAM77>	Drag 41	LD74	unphased		[238]	incised
<SAM78>	large enclosed form	LD74	unphased		[F18]	incised
<SAM79>	large enclosed form	LD74	8	OA9	[224]	incised

LD76 [736]
<SAM10>, Fig 17, (also LD76 [284], [721], unphased LD74 [F31]) Drag 37. Lezoux. A straight line beneath the ovolo was used by several potters, and this ovolo is shown with such a line on *SS* pl 55, no. 23, attributed to Pugnus. The large spray of feather-motifs in the medallion occurs with a Pugnus ovolo on *SS* pl 155, no. 25, and on a bowl from Silchester (May 1916, pl 26, no. 24), while the partial impression of motifs to fill corners, as here where the angles of the medallion panels contain a small leaf from a tree (Rogers 1974, N2), seems to be a feature of Pugnus's work. There is no apparent parallel for the ?double-headed arrow in the festoon, but cf the incomplete motif on *SS* pl 155, no. 25, which has an arrow terminal. The figure is probably Oswald 570. *c* AD 145–75. Rivet-repaired; the sherd from LD76 [721] is burnt.
<SAM64> see LD76 [629] Drag 37. Rheinzabern.
Drag 31, CG, Antonine. Drag 18/31, CG, early 2nd century. Drag 18/31 or 31, EG, Antonine. Drag 32, EG, later 2nd–mid 3rd century. EG sherd.

LD76 [743]
Drag 37, CG, top of ovolo, Antonine.

LD76 [1055]
Drag 27, SG, Flavian–Trajanic.

LD76 [1060]
Drag 18/31, CG, Hadrianic–Antonine.

LD76 [1403]
Two Drag 18, SG, pre- to early Flavian.

LD76 [1244]
Drag 27, CG, early 2nd century.

LD76 [1305]
<SAM3>, Fig 17, Drag 37. La Graufesenque. Panel design, including a saltire with leaves and triple poppyheads (cf Hermet 1934, pl 64, no. 21) and a vertical row of chevrons; basal wreath of leaves, as Atkinson 1914, pl 15, no. 76. *c* AD 70–90.
Drag 18, SG, second half 1st century. Drag 18?, SG, Neronian–early Flavian.

Phase 5 Open Area 5

LD76 [189]
Drag 32, EG, later 2nd–mid 3rd century (probably one vessel); slightly burnt. Drag 37, EG, later 2nd–mid 3rd century.

LD76 [354]
Mortarium, EG, late 2nd–mid 3rd century.

LD76 [728]
Wa 79, CG, later 2nd century.

LD76 [758]
Drag 33, CG, Antonine.

LD76 [1017]
Drag 18/31, CG, Antonine. CG sherd. Drag 37, EG, fragment of decoration; later 2nd–mid 3rd century.

LD76 [1073]
Drag 18, SG, Flavian–Trajanic.

LD76 [1205]
EG sherd.

Phase 6 Building 1

LD76 [301]
<SAM26>, Fig 18, Drag 37. Trier. The ovolo, here with traces of a guideline, was used by Criciro (Oelmann 1914, Taf 6, no. 21); the motif beneath is not identifiable. *c* AD 190–210.

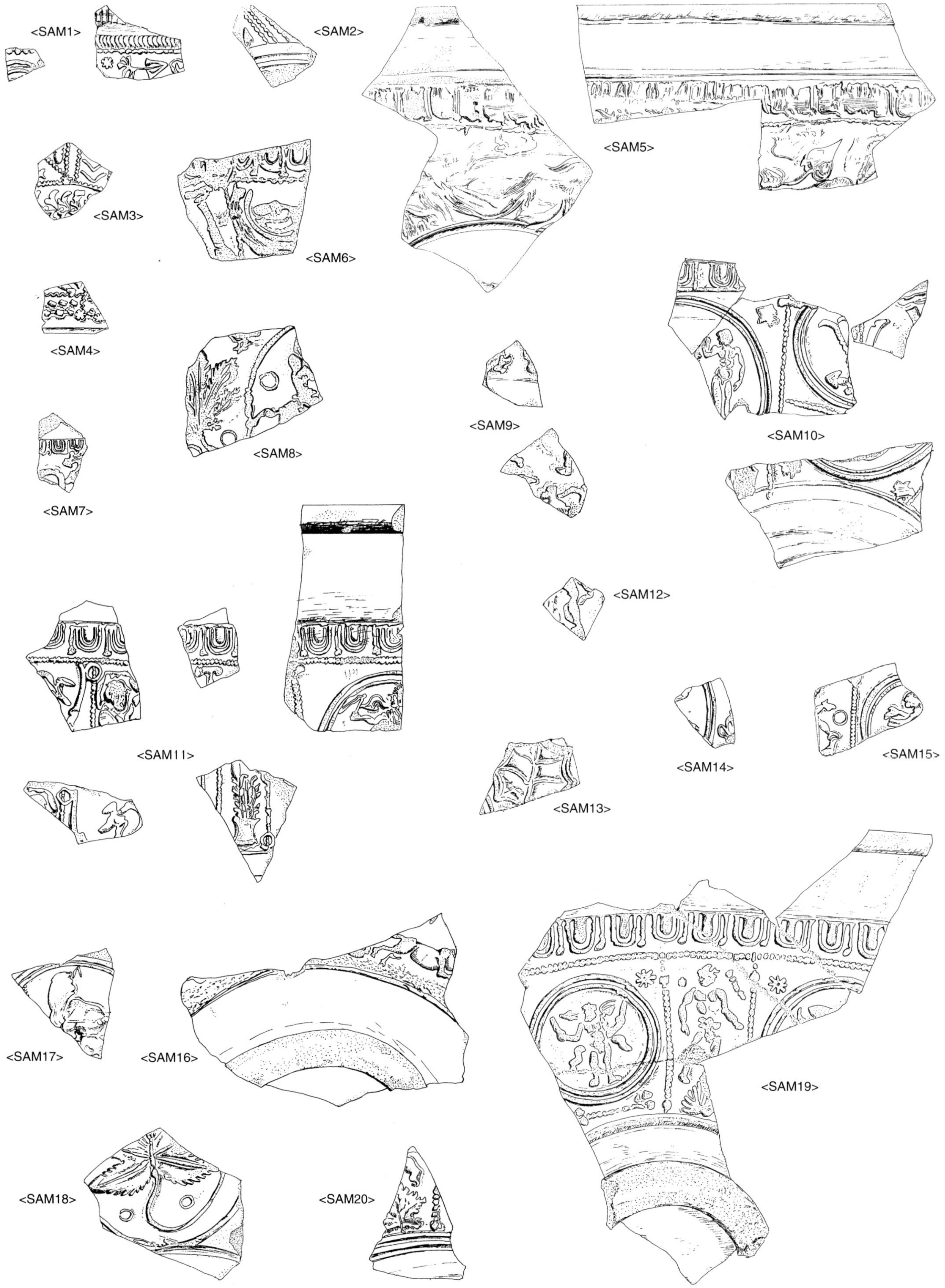

Fig 17 *Decorated samian from La Graufesenque <SAM1>–<SAM5>; Montans <SAM6>; Les Martres-de-Veyre <SAM7> and Lezoux <SAM8>–<SAM20> (scale 1:2)*

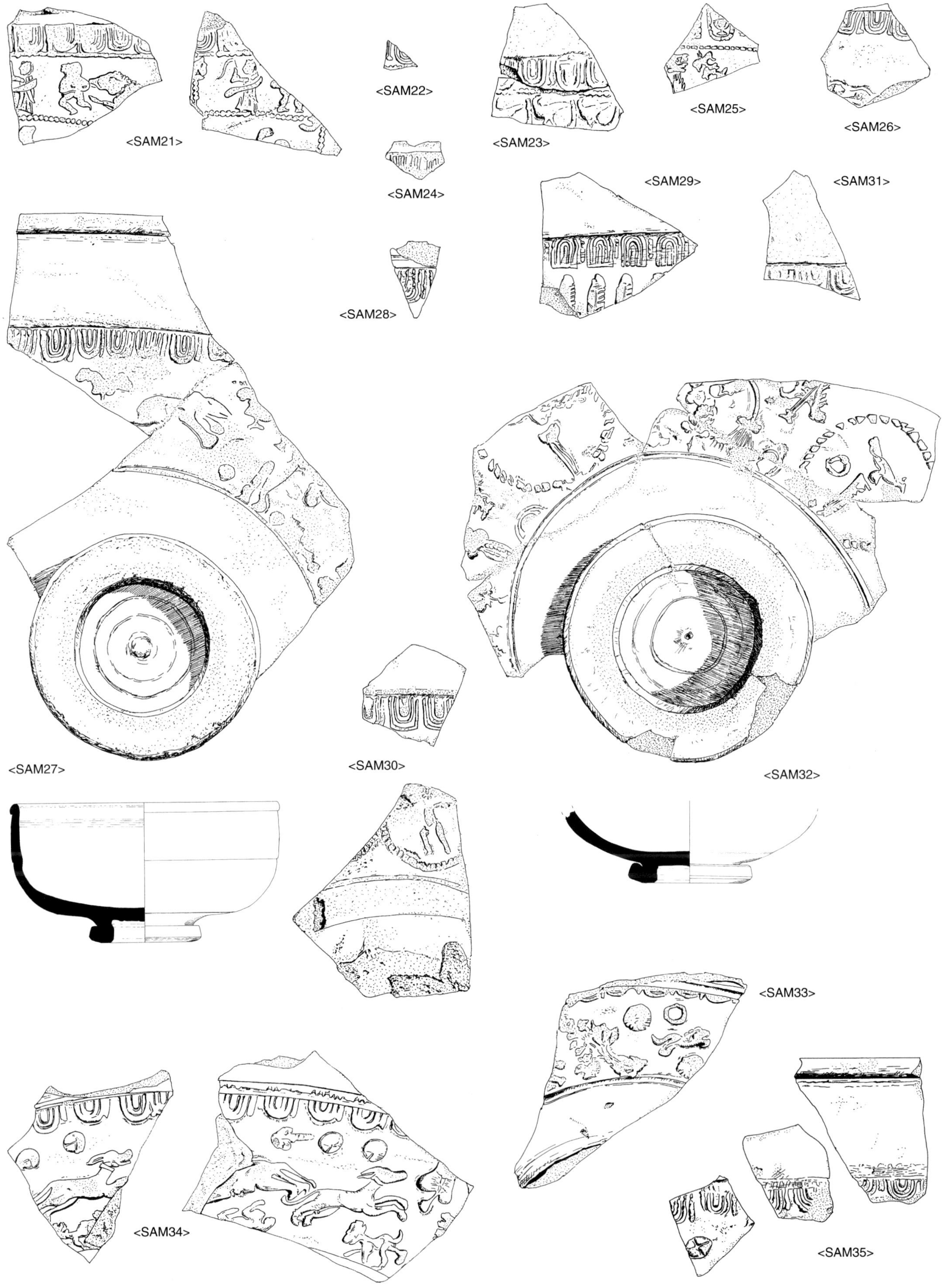

Fig 18 Decorated samian from La Madeleine *<SAM21>*; Lavoye *<SAM22>* and Trier *<SAM23>*–*<SAM35>* (scale: sherds 1:2, reconstructed profiles 1:4)

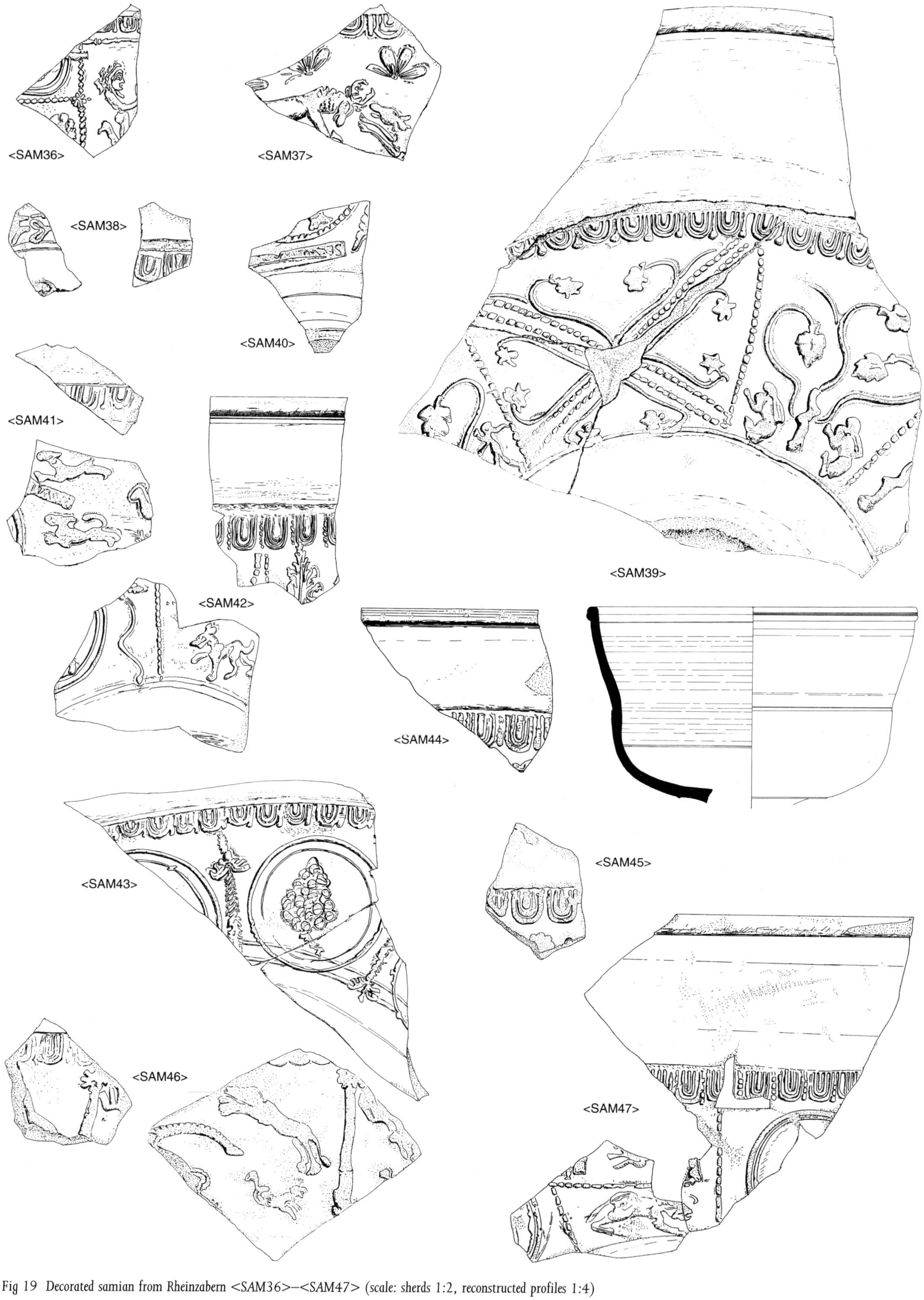

Fig 19 Decorated samian from Rheinzabern *<SAM36>–<SAM47>* (scale: sherds 1:2, reconstructed profiles 1:4)

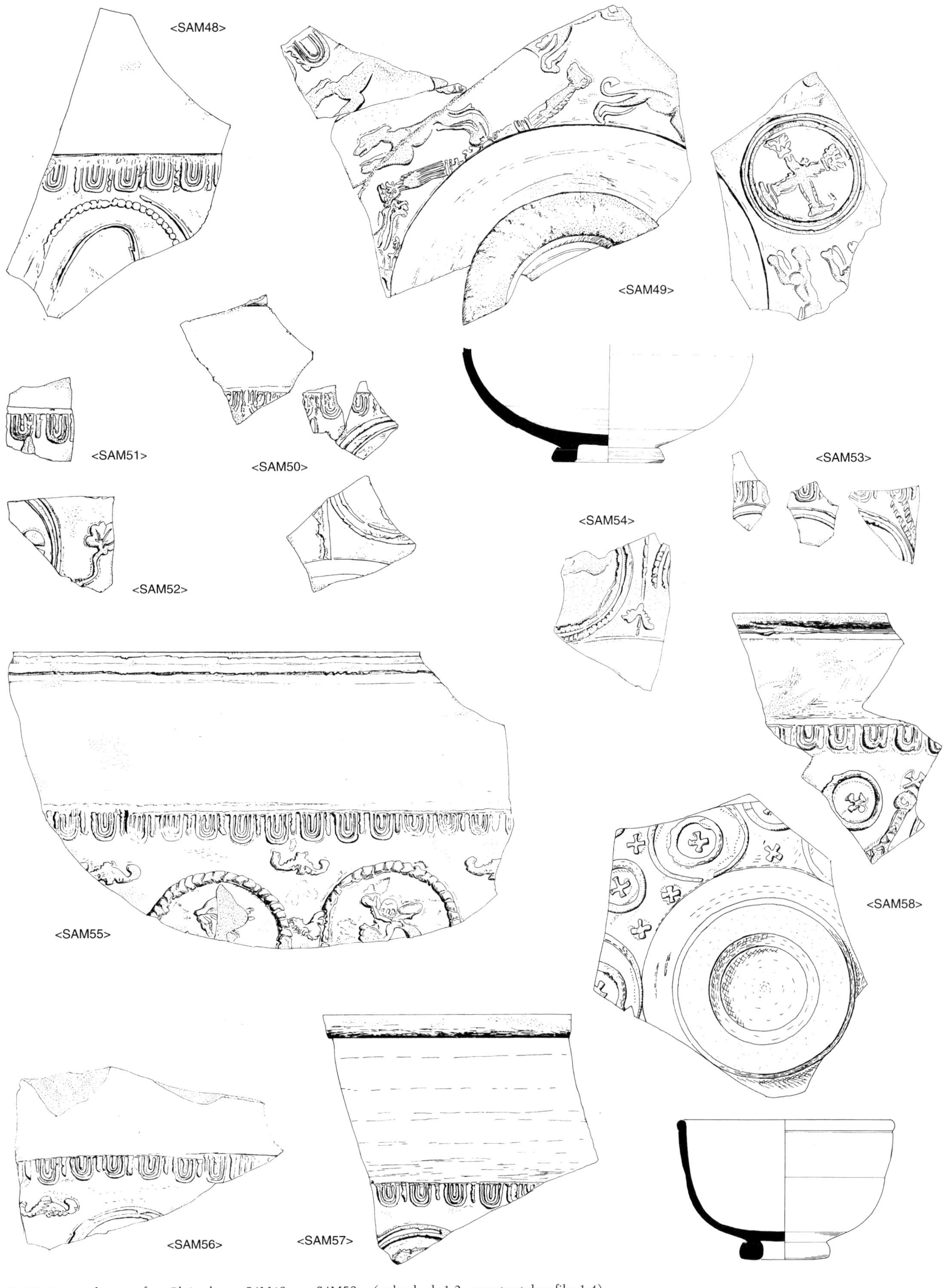

Fig 20 Decorated samian from Rheinzabern *<SAM48>–<SAM58>* (scale: sherds 1:2, reconstructed profiles 1:4)

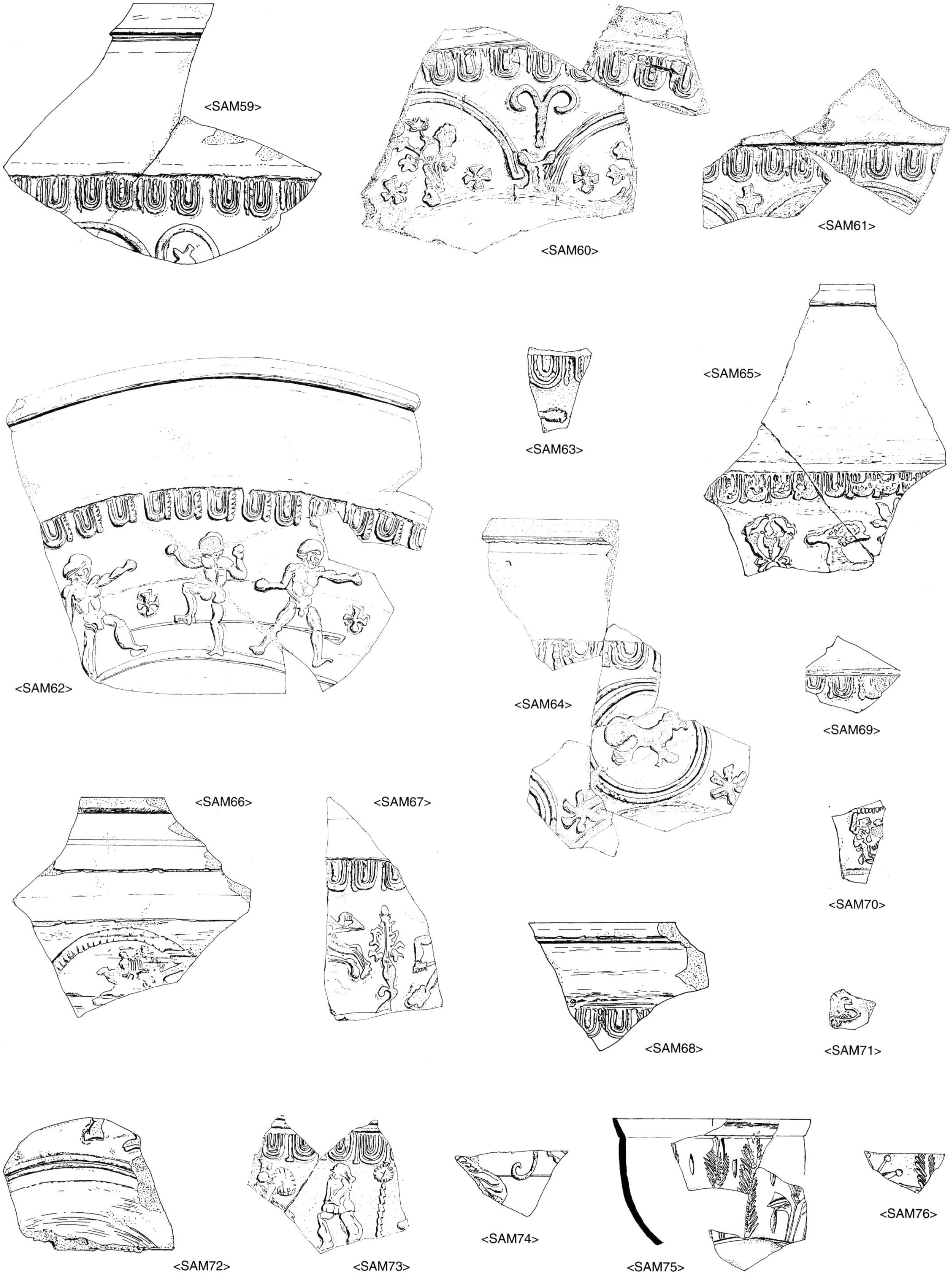

Fig 21 *Decorated samian from Rheinzabern <SAM59>–<SAM72>; Colchester <SAM73>; Central Gaul <SAM74> and incised cups from Rheinzabern <SAM75>–<SAM76> (scale: sherds 1:2, reconstructed profiles 1:4)*

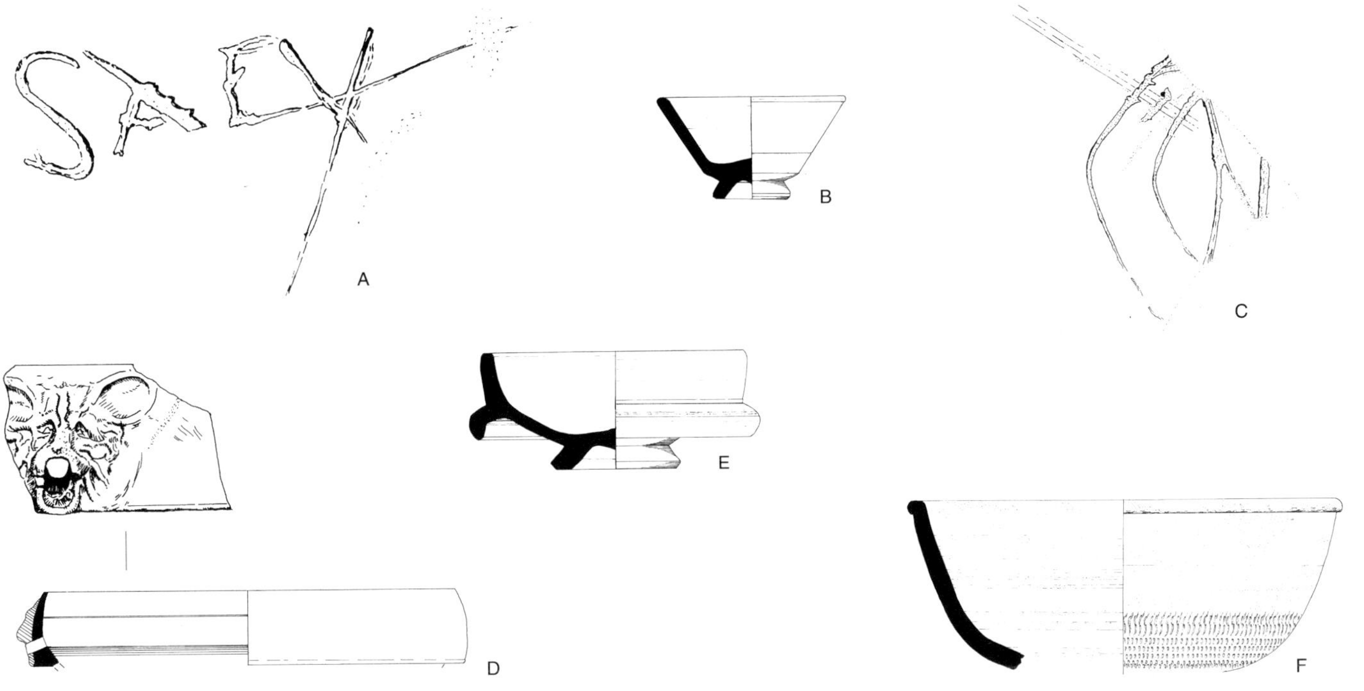

Fig 22 Graffiti on samian (A, unphased LD74 [171.1], scale 2:1; C, unphased LD74 [232], scale 1:1) and samian plain wares (B, unphased LD74 [186]; D, phase 10 OA11 LD76 [78]; E, phase 6 S4 LD76 [361]; F, phase 6 S4 LD76 [365] and [383]; all scale 1:4 except detail of lion-head spout on D 1:2)

LD76 [700]
<SAM5> see LD76 [361] Drag 37. La Graufesenque.
<SAM58>, Fig 20, (also unphased LD76 [22], LD74 [+]) Drag 37. Rheinzabern. In the style of Julius II–Julianus I, with mould-stamp of Julius II (<STAMP2>, Fig 23). The ovolo, *RF*.E45, medallions K7 and K14, cross O53 and stamp are recorded on closely similar bowls, such as *LR* Taf 204, nos 5, 10, 20. *c* AD 225–50. The band between rim and decoration is 35mm high, the footring heavy and square. EG dish sherd.

LD74 [293]
Drag 31/Lud Sa, EG, later 2nd–mid 3rd century.

Phase 6 Open Area 7

LD74 [295]
Déch 67 probably, CG, early 2nd century.

LD74 [303]
<SAM12>, Fig 17, Drag 37. Lezoux. The figure is probably Diana, *Oswald* 111, used by Cinnamus. Antonine.
Drag 45, EG, later 2nd–mid 3rd century, worn inside. Drag 38, EG, later 2nd–mid 3rd century, four notches cut on top of flange. EG sherd.

Phase 6 Structure 4

LD76 [146]
Drag 32, EG, later 2nd–mid 3rd century. Closed form, EG, later 2nd–mid 3rd century.

LD76 [261]
<SAM47>, Fig 19, (also LD76 [648] [649] [657], LD74 [19]) Drag 37. Rheinzabern. In the style of Verecundus II, who used all the motifs: the ovolo *RF*.E10, bear T62a, stag T93a, medallion K19a, arch KB95 and beadrow O260. The redrawing or guideline for the medallion is characteristic: cf *LR* Tafn 169, no. 5; 170, no. 17; 172, no. 8; 173, no. 3; for the general style, cf Tafn 169–70. First half 3rd century. The band between rim and decoration is 50mm high.
<SAM57>, Fig 20, Drag 37. Rheinzabern. In the style of Primitivus IV, with his ovolo, *RF*.E41; the motif in the medallion K19 may be a bird, T244, as *LR* Taf 201, no. 3. Early to mid 3rd century. The band between rim and decoration is 55mm high.
Drag 31R/Lud Sb, EG, later 2nd–mid 3rd century. Two Drag 30 or 37, CG, Antonine.

LD76 [270]
Drag 31?, CG, Antonine.

LD76 [272]
Drag 37, CG, tip of ovolo, Antonine.

LD76 [278]
<SAM13>, Fig 17, Drag 30. Lezoux. Scroll with a large leaf, Rogers 1974, J1, used by several potters, including Cinnamus and Doeccus. Antonine.
Drag 31R/Lud Sb, EG, later 2nd–mid 3rd century.

LD76 [284]
<SAM10> see LD76 [736], Drag 37. Lezoux.

LD76 [327]
<SAM22>, Fig 18, Drag 37. Lavoye. The broken ovolo is probably *Oswald* 1945, fig 6, i, used by Gesatus. Early to mid Antonine.
<SAM56>, Fig 20, Drag 37. Rheinzabern. In the style of Primitivus IV, with ovolo *RF*.E41, large acanthus P113 and medallion K19. Early to mid 3rd century.
Drag 18/31, CG, Hadrianic.

LD76 [357]
<SAM52>, Fig 20, Drag 37. Rheinzabern. In the style of Primitivus I, who used the leaf, *RF*.P83, on a similar tendril beside the medallion K19a: *LR* Taf 190, no. 10. The ovolo may be E40; the motif in the medallion is not identifiable. Early to mid 3rd century.
<SAM65>, Fig 21, Drag 37. Rheinzabern. In the style of Perpetuus. The motifs – ovolo, *RF*.E17, stag T90b, rosette O34a and cornucopia O160b – are on *LR* Taf 237, no. 12, which is from a closely similar mould. Second quarter 3rd century, probably. The band between rim and decoration is 65mm high.
Drag 32, EG, later 2nd–mid 3rd century. CG sherd, probably Drag 38; Antonine

LD76 [358]
Drag 31R/Lud Sb, EG, later 2nd–mid 3rd century.

LD76 [360]
<SAM2>, Fig 17, Drag 29. La Graufesenque. Base of the lower zone, with diagonal wavy lines over massed leaf tips. *c* AD 70–85.

<SAM43>, Fig 19, (also unphased LD76 [144]) Drag 37. Rheinzabern. In the style of Lupus, apparently the only user of the small corded motif RF.O235 used here as a stalk for the grapes. The other motifs – ovolo E46, grapes P164, acanthus P145, feathered vertical O273 and double medallion K20 – were shared by Julius I, but the double line at the base seems to be a regular feature of Lupus's bowls (eg *LR* Taf 157, nos 1, 7, 9). First half 3rd century.
Drag 18, probably 18R; SG, Flavian–Trajanic.

LD76 [361]
<SAM5>, Fig 17, (also LD76 [700] [751] and unphased LD74 [F33A] [F29]; LD76 [80] [233] [721]) Drag 37. La Graufesenque. The bowl has shifted in the mould while still soft, smearing the whole decorative frieze which has then been smoothed over. The details are now very unclear: the ovolo is probably that on Grimes 1930, fig 34, no. 14, while the main frieze consists of a scroll of pointed frilled leaves with an unidentifiable motif, perhaps a small bird, in the field. *c* AD 90–110. Such overall damage to the decoration is rare: while some smudging is occasionally seen on the lower zones of Drag 29, it is due to the longer drying time needed below the carination, and does not affect the whole bowl. A Drag 37 of similar date from the Montans pottery, its decoration completely removed below the ovolo, is discussed by Tilhard (1998).
<SAM55>, Fig 20 (also LD76 [659]) Drag 37. Rheinzabern. In the style of Primitivus IV, the only recorded user of the ovolo, RF.E41, medallion K37 and small acanthus P146; he also used the large acanthus P113, cupid M111a and cornucopia O160a. Early to mid 3rd century. The band between rim and decoration is 55mm high.
Drag 38, Fig 22E, EG, later 2nd–mid 3rd century; unstamped (also LD76 [383]). Drag 32, EG, later 2nd–mid 3rd century (probably one vessel, but possibly two). Two Drag 33, CG, Antonine. Drag 31/37, rouletted on exterior (as Oswald and Pryce 1920, pl 75, nos 10, 12); EG, later 2nd–mid 3rd century. Drag 37, EG, later 2nd–mid 3rd century. Two Drag 31/Lud Sa, EG, later 2nd–mid 3rd century. Two Drag 31R, CG, later Antonine. Drag 31R/Lud Sb, EG, later 2nd–mid 3rd century. Drag 18/31, SG, Flavian–Trajanic. One SG sherd. One EG sherd.

LD76 [362]
Drag 37, CG, Hadrianic–early Antonine. Drag 31, CG, Antonine.

LD76 [363]
Drag 32, EG, later 2nd–mid 3rd century. Drag 33, CG, Antonine.

LD76 [364]
Drag 33, CG, Antonine. Drag 37 probably, CG, Hadrianic–early Antonine. Drag 37, EG, top of ovolo; late 2nd–mid 3rd century.

LD76 [365]
Drag 31/37, Fig 22F, rouletted on exterior (as Oswald and Pryce 1920, pl 75, nos 10, 12); EG, later 2nd–mid 3rd century.

LD76 [368]
EG sherd, probably Drag 32, later 2nd–mid 3rd century.

LD76 [370]
<SAM50>, Fig 20 (also LD76 [1438], unphased LD74 [F29]) Drag 37. Rheinzabern. Only Attillus seems to have used both the ovolo, RF.E40, and medallion K20; the vertical is probably O239. First half 3rd century. The band between rim and decoration is 35mm high.
Two Drag 33, CG, Antonine. Drag 31R, CG, later 2nd century. Rouletted base sherd, dish, CG.

LD76 [383]
Drag 38, Fig 22E, EG, later 2nd–mid 3rd century (also LD76 [361]).

LD76 [527]
CG sherd, Drag 31R, later 2nd century.

LD76 [628]
Drag 38, EG, late 2nd–mid 3rd century. SG sherd, probably Drag 18, later 1st century.

LD76 [640]
Drag 31R, CG, mid–late Antonine; very worn under the base.

LD76 [645]
<SAM1> see LD76 [710]) Drag 29. La Graufesenque.
<SAM59> see LD76 [307] Drag 37. Rheinzabern. Drag 37 or 30, EG, later 2nd–mid 3rd century. Drag 31/Lud Sa, EG, later 2nd–mid 3rd century. Drag 32 probably, EG, later 2nd–mid 3rd century. EG footring. One EG sherd. Drag 38 probably, EG, later 2nd–mid 3rd century.

LD76 [648]
<SAM47> see LD76 [261] Drag 37. Rheinzabern.
<SAM59> see LD76 [307] Drag 37. Rheinzabern.
Two mortarium sherds, EG, later 2nd–mid 3rd century; worn inside. Mortarium base, EG, late 2nd–mid 3rd century; worn inside. One EG sherd. One CG sherd. Drag 37, CG, fragment of ovolo and beadrow; Antonine.

LD76 [649]
<SAM47> see LD76 [261] Drag 37. Rheinzabern.
Drag 37 foot, EG, first half 3rd century.

LD76 [651]
<SAM62>, Fig 21, (also LD76 [657]) Drag 37. Rheinzabern. In the style of Julius II–Julianus I, who used the ovolo, RF.E45, cross O53 and pugilists M191 and M194: cf *LR* Taf 211, nos 2, 3; Bird 1986, no. 2.111. For the guidelines, cf Taf 209, nos 3, 9, 14. *c* AD 225–50. The band between rim and decoration is 45mm high.
Drag 33, EG, later 2nd–mid 3rd century. Drag 30, CG, mid–late Antonine. Drag 30 or 37, CG, Antonine. Drag 36, EG, later 2nd–mid 3rd century. Three EG sherds, probably Drag 37, with trace of moulded decoration. Two Drag 31/Lud Sa, EG, later 2nd–mid 3rd century. EG mortarium sherd, heavily worn inside; late 2nd–mid 3rd century. One CG sherd. One EG sherd.

LD76 [656]
Two Drag 38, EG, later 2nd–mid 3rd century. Drag 32, EG, later 2nd–mid 3rd century.

LD76 [657]
<SAM47> see LD76 [261] Drag 37. Rheinzabern.
<SAM62> see LD76 [651] Drag 37. Rheinzabern.
Drag 31R/Lud Sb, EG, later 2nd–mid 3rd century. Drag 38, EG, later 2nd–mid 3rd century. Drag 33, EG, later 2nd–mid 3rd century. Foot, Drag 31R/Lud Sb, EG, later 2nd–mid 3rd century. 3 EG sherds and one footring fragment.

LD76 [659]
<SAM55> see LD76 [361] Drag 37. Rheinzabern.
<SAM71>, Fig 21, Drag 37. Rheinzabern. Leaf RF.P75a. Later 2nd century to first half 3rd.
Cu 15, CG, Antonine. Drag 32, EG, later 2nd–mid 3rd century. Drag 33, CG, Antonine.

LD76 [667]
Drag 37 foot, EG, second quarter 3rd century. EG mortarium base, late 2nd–mid 3rd century; worn inside and slightly burnt. EG sherd.

Phase 6 Structure 6

LD74 [305]
Drag 30 or 37, EG, later 2nd–mid 3rd century.

Phase 6 Structure 7

LD74 [291]
Drag 18/31, CG, Hadrianic–Antonine.

Phase 7 Open Area 8

LD76 [255]
<SAM59> see LD76 [307] Drag 37. Rheinzabern.
<SAM60>, Fig 21, (also unphased LD74 [186]) Drag 37. Rheinzabern. In the style of Julius II–Julianus I, who used the ovolo, RF.E23, cross O53, tree P2a, rams-horn O156, altar O179 and arcade KB73. For similar bowls, cf *LR* Tafn 205, nos 3, 14; 206, no. 14. *c* AD 225–50.

Phase 7 Structure 8

LD76 [240]
<SAM46>, Fig 19, (also LD74 [169], unphased)
Drag 37. Rheinzabern. In the style of Victorinus I, the sole recorded user of ovolo RF.E16; he also used the arcade KB122,

hound T130a, seahorse T190f, rosette O48 and vertical O274; the other animal may be his hare, T162.
Cf *LR* Tafn 166, no. 1; 167, nos 1, 9. Early to mid 3rd century.

LD76 [228]
Drag 37, EG, later 2nd–mid 3rd century. Drag 38, CG, mid–late Antonine. Drag 38 probably, CG, Antonine. Drag 33, CG, Hadrianic–Antonine. Mortarium or Cu 21, CG, late 2nd century. EG sherd.

LD76 [303]
Drag 33, EG, later 2nd–mid 3rd century. Drag 31 or 31R, CG, mid–later Antonine.

LD76 [308]
CG sherd, second half 2nd century.

LD74 [18]
<SAM29>, Fig 18, Drag 37. Trier. In the style of Afer. The ovolo and leaf are in the same arrangement on Gard 1937, Taf 14, no. 12. *c* AD 200–220.
<SAM27>, Fig 18, (also LD74 [4.1], unphased [232]) Drag 37. Trier. In the style of Criciro. The ovolo was used with the bear and with the cockerel on Oelmann 1914, Taf 6, nos 19, 21, and with the cockerel and rosette on Bird 1986, no. 2.71. The figure is a captive, Fölzer 1913, type 516. *c* AD 190–210. The bowl comes from a worn mould; the band between rim and decoration is 35mm high, the footring heavy and square.
<SAM41>, Fig 19, (also unphased LD74 [3]) Drag 37. Rheinzabern. With mould stamp of Comitialis (<STAMP1>, Fig 23), in the style of Comitialis V. *LR* Taf 98, no. 4, is probably from the same mould and has the ovolo *RF*.E17, archer M174, hound T139, leaf P38 and double medallion K19. *c* AD 175–220.
<SAM42>, Fig 19, (also LD74 [4.3], [19], unphased LD74 [1]) Drag 37. Rheinzabern. In the style of Comitialis VI. All the motifs are found in his work: the ovolo *RF*.E25, dog T138a, leaf P75a, medallion K19, festoon KB95 and beadrow O263. The motif in the medallion may be a cupid, M111, as on a similar bowl (*LR* Taf 104, no. 7) which shares most of the motifs and a similar tendril. The square edge beneath the ovolo may be the end of a mould stamp. *c* AD 175–220. The band between rim and decoration is 35mm high.
<SAM49>, Fig 20, (also LD74 [4.3] [19] [67]) Drag 37. Rheinzabern. In the style of Helenius, who used the ovolo and line, *RF*.E7, column O6, medallion K19a, hound T135 and hare T153; the lion is a slightly larger version of T20, which he also used. For the crossed columns, see *LR* Taf 175, no. 2; for the general style, Taf 177. Early to mid 3rd century. The footring is heavy and square.
<SAM75>, Fig 21, (also unphased LD74 [4]) Drag 41. Rheinzabern. With incised vertical palm branches and delicate ears of barley. The palm branch occurs on this form with a variety of other foliage and geometric motifs: Oswald and Pryce 1920, pl 78, nos 1, 8; Schulz and Schellenberger 1996, Abb 70. Early to mid 3rd century.
Drag 37, EG, later 2nd–mid 3rd century. Drag 38, EG, later 2nd–mid 3rd century, very abraded. Drag 45, EG, late 2nd–mid 3rd century. Drag 32, EG, later 2nd–mid 3rd century. Two Drag 37 rims, probably, EG, later 2nd–mid 3rd century. Three Drag 31/Lud Sa, EG, later 2nd–mid 3rd century. Drag 37 sherd, EG, tip of abraded ovolo, later 2nd–mid 3rd century. Drag 31, CG, Antonine. EG sherd. Two CG sherds.

LD74 [266]
Two Drag 38, CG, later 2nd–mid 3rd century. Drag 37 base, EG (Trier), second quarter 3rd century. Drag 31/33 (no bead at rim), EG, later 2nd–mid 3rd century. EG bowl sherd.

Phase 7 Structure 9

LD76 [1445]
Drag 33, EG, later 2nd–mid 3rd century.

LD74 [19]
<SAM37>, Fig 19, Drag 37. Rheinzabern. Probably to be attributed to Cerialis, who used the ovolo, *RF*.E3, stag T84 and the rosette O37 fully impressed. The hound is T133; the broken motif is probably a peacock, T227, also recorded for Cerialis. *c* AD 170–200.
<SAM42> see LD74 [18] Drag 37. Rheinzabern.
<SAM47> see LD76 [261] Drag 37. Rheinzabern.
<SAM49> see LD74 [18] Drag 37. Rheinzabern.
<SAM70>, Fig 21, Drag 37. Rheinzabern. Mask *RF*.M9. Later 2nd century to first half 3rd.
Drag 30, EG, later 2nd–mid 3rd century. Drag 45, EG, late 2nd–mid 3rd century. Two Drag 31/Lud Sa, EG, later 2nd–mid 3rd century. Cu 21, CG, later 2nd century. Drag 30 or 37, EG, later 2nd–mid 3rd century. Drag 38, EG, later 2nd–mid 3rd century. Nine EG sherds. Drag 37, EG, top of ovolo, later 2nd–mid 3rd century.

Phase 8 Open Area 9

LD74 [4.2]
Drag 38 probably, EG, later 2nd–mid 3rd century. Drag 31/Lud Sa, EG, later 2nd–mid 3rd century.

LD74 [4.3]
<SAM19>, Fig 17, (also LD76 [201] unphased [4.4]) Drag 37. Lezoux. In the style of Doeccus. The ovolo is Rogers 1974, B227/235, assigned to Doeccus and an associated potter, Ollognatus. The other motifs are all illustrated in *SS*: the cupid, *Oswald* 450 variant, is on pl 148, no. 24, the faun *Oswald* 717 on pl 150, no. 52, the four-beaded rosette and the astragalus on pl 151, no. 62, and the beadrows and eight-bladed rosette on pl 148, no. 22; the frilled leaf is probably that on pl 150, no. 43. *c* AD 165–200.
<SAM42> see LD74 [18] Drag 37. Rheinzabern.
<SAM49> see LD74 [18] Drag 37. Rheinzabern.
Drag 31, CG, Antonine. Two Drag 31/Lud Sa or Sb, EG, later 2nd–mid 3rd century. Two Drag 37 probably, EG, later 2nd–mid 3rd century. Two Drag 45, EG, late 2nd–mid 3rd century, one very abraded. Three EG sherds. Drag 37, EG, fragment of decoration, later 2nd–mid 3rd century.

LD74 [195.1]
Drag 33, EG, later 2nd–mid 3rd century.

LD74 [197]
<SAM4>, Fig 17, Knorr 78. La Graufesenque. Panel design, including a small animal over a double row of leaf tips and a vertical band of rosettes: cf Hermet 1934, pl 92, nos 21, 23. *c* AD 75–95.
<SAM33>, Fig 18, Drag 37. Trier. In the style of Dubitatus–Dubitus. The ovolo, tree, lion and probably the same rosette are on Simon and Köhler 1992, Taf 27, no. C I 156; for the ovolo, rosette and ring, see Gard 1937, Taf 23, no. 7. *c* AD 225–45.
<SAM67>, Fig 21, Drag 37. Rheinzabern. In the style of Regulinus, who used the ovolo, *RF*.E26, gladiator M226a, boar T66 and leaf P75b, and the leaf on a tendril P108 of which he was apparently the sole user. Cf *LR* Taf 242, nos 5, 7, 12. Second quarter 3rd century, probably.
Drag 37, EG, later 2nd–mid 3rd century. Drag 33, EG, later 2nd–mid 3rd century. Drag 31/Lud Sa, EG, later 2nd–mid 3rd century. Base, probably from a flagon or large beaker, foot as Lud Ka, Chenet 335; EG (Argonne), later 2nd–4th century. Drag 37, EG, fragment of decoration, later 2nd–mid 3rd century.

LD74 [199]
Cu 21 (as Oswald and Pryce 1920, pl 73, no. 4) or Chenet 324h, EG (Argonne), later 2nd–4th century. Drag 38, EG, later 2nd–mid 3rd century, worn inside. Two Drag 31/Lud Sa, EG, later 2nd–mid 3rd century. Mortarium sherd, EG, later 2nd–mid 3rd century.

LD74 [201]
<SAM19> see LD76 [4.3] Drag 37. Lezoux.
Drag 37, EG, later 2nd–mid 3rd century. Drag 38, EG, later 2nd–mid 3rd century.

LD74 [219.1]
Drag 31R/Lud Sb, EG, later 2nd–mid 3rd century, worn foot. CG sherd.

LD74 [219.2]
Drag 31/Lud Sa, EG, later 2nd–mid 3rd century.

LD74 [219.3]
EG sherd.

LD74 [219.5]
CG sherd.

LD74 [224]
<SAM79> Large enclosed form with incised foliage motifs. Rheinzabern. Later 2nd–first half 3rd century. CG sherd. Drag 33, CG, Antonine. Drag 30 or 37, EG, later 2nd–mid 3rd century. EG sherd.

LD74 [233.2]
<SAM61>, Fig 21, (also LD74 [255]) Drag 37. Rheinzabern. In the style of Julius II–Julianus I: *LR* Taf 207, nos 10, 12, have all the motifs – ovolo *RF*.E23, cross O53 and double arcade KB80 – in the same arrangement. *c* AD 225–50. (LD74 [F233B], [F255])

LD74 [255]
<SAM61> see LD74 [233.2] Drag 37. Rheinzabern. Two Drag 30 or 37 rims, EG, later 2nd–mid 3rd century. Drag 37 base, CG, Antonine. Drag 45, EG, later 2nd–mid 3rd century. Large jar (as Lud VMg, Vse), EG, later 2nd–mid 3rd century.

Phase 9 Open Area 10

LD76 [732]
<SAM59> see LD76 [307] Drag 37. Rheinzabern .
Drag 37, EG, later 2nd–mid 3rd century.

LD76 [1277]
Drag 33, EG, early–mid 3rd century.

LD74 [1]
Drag 31, CG, Antonine.

LD74 [2]
<SAM20>, Fig 17, Drag 37. Lezoux. In the style of Doeccus. The figure is probably the cupid shown with the same leaf and beadrow on *SS* pl 150, no. 47; the terminal is on pl 150, no. 48. *c* AD 165–200.
<SAM38>, Fig 19, (also unphased LD74 [+]) (Probably one bowl) Drag 37. Rheinzabern. Arvernicus–Lutaevus used the ovolo, *RF*.E2, and was apparently the only user of R33 as a basal wreath. *c* AD 170–200.
Drag 37, CG, Hadrianic–early Antonine. Mortarium sherd, EG, later 2nd–mid 3rd century.

LD74 [4]
Drag 18, SG, second half of 1st century. Drag 37 or 30, CG, Antonine. One CG sherd. One EG sherd.

LD74 [4.1]
<SAM27> see LD74 [18] Drag 37. Trier.
<SAM53>, Fig 20, Drag 30. Rheinzabern. In the style of Primitivus I. The ovolo *RF*. E40, medallion K19a and corded line O242 are in a similar arrangement on *LR* Taf 190, no. 9. Early–mid 3rd century.
Rim, Drag 45 probably, EG, later 2nd–mid 3rd century, very abraded.

LD74 [114]
<SAM23>, Fig 18, Drag 37. Trier. Werkstatt I, Stufe A. Huld–Zetsche 1972, Taf 3, A17, has the ovolo and the frieze of birds between the stems of leaves, and may be from the same mould. Hadrianic–early Antonine. Very abraded, with no slip surviving.
<SAM72>, Fig 21, Drag 37. Rheinzabern. With a column or broad beadrow and perhaps an altar motif at the base. Later 2nd–first half 3rd century.
Drag 37, EG, later 2nd–mid 3rd century. EG sherd.

LD74 [114.1]
One CG sherd, one EG sherd (probably Argonne and later 2nd–4th century).

LD74 [114]
<SAM30>, Fig 18 (also LD74 [1], unphased) (Probably one bowl) Drag 37. Trier. In the style of Afer. The ovolo is on Bird 1986, no. 2.72; for the cupid and cogged medallion, see Bird 1986, no. 2.75, by Afer-Marinus. *c* AD 200–20. Three EG sherds, two of them very worn.

Phase 10 Open Area 11

LD76 [50]
EG sherd.

LD76 [51]
Drag 45, EG, later 2nd–mid 3rd century.

LD76 [62]
<SAM35>, Fig 18, (also unphased LD74 [251.1] [285]) (Probably one bowl) Drag 37. Trier. In the style of the Primanus group. Ovolo and rosette, as Bird 1986, no. 2.87. *c* AD 235–50. The band between rim and decoration is 35mm high.
Dish, Drag 32 probably, EG, later 2nd–mid 3rd century. Drag 33, EG, later 2nd–mid 3rd century.

LD76 [78]
Drag 45, Fig 22D, with lion-head spout; EG (Rheinzabern), later 2nd–mid 3rd century, slightly burnt. Drag 33, EG, later 2nd–mid 3rd century. Drag 30 or 37, EG later 2nd–mid 3rd century. Rim fragment, probably Drag 30 or 37, EG. Drag 32 EG, later 2nd–mid 3rd century. Two EG sherds.

LD76 [86]
Closed form, EG, later 2nd–mid 3rd century. CG sherd, Hadrianic–Antonine.

LD76 [185]
Drag 38 probably, EG, later 2nd–mid 3rd century.

LD76 [186]
<SAM60> see LD74 [255] Drag 37. Rheinzabern.
Jar/large beaker sherd, EG, later 2nd–mid 3rd century.

LD76 [285]
<SAM74>, Fig 21, (also unphased LD76 [646]) Large jar or beaker with applied motif, probably a leaf, and barbotine tendrils. Central Gaul, Antonine.

LD76 [309]
Drag 37 base, EG (Trier), late 2nd–mid 3rd century. EG sherd, probably from base of a second Trier Drag 37, later 2nd–mid 3rd century. Drag 27, SG, Flavian. Four CG sherds, including one from a Drag 31, Antonine.

LD76 [751]
<SAM5> see LD76 [361] Drag 37. La Graufesenque.
SG sherd, second half 1st century.

LD76 [1240]
Drag 33, EG, later 2nd–early 3rd century.

LD76 [1461]
Drag 31R/Lud Sb, EG, later 2nd–mid 3rd century. Drag 27 or 35 CG, Trajanic–Hadrianic. Drag 37 EG, fragment of double medallion, later 2nd–mid 3rd century.

Unphased

LD74 [4.3]
<SAM24>, Fig 18, Drag 37. Trier. The incomplete ovolo has a hollow core, as several of the ovolos shared by Werkstatt I and II. Hadrianic–Antonine.

LD74 [4.4]
<SAM25>, Fig 18, (also unphased LD74 [1]) Drag 37. Trier. In the style of Dexter. Fölzer 1913, Taf 15, no. 14, has the vase ovolo, wreath festoon and column, no. 39 the beadrow. *c* AD 160–90.

LD74 [22.2]
<SAM21>, Fig 18, Drag 37. La Madeleine. In the style 'Ware mit Eierstab Cb'. The ovolo, here partially cramped, is Ricken 1934, Taf 7, C, and the figure with raised arm is probably Taf 7, type 90. The figure with a whip, the bifid leaf and the beadrow are on Taf 9, no. 15, the large rosette on Taf 9, no. 6. There are apparently no close parallels for the two gladiators or the bear. Hadrianic–early Antonine.

LD74 [171.1]
<SAM51>, Fig 20, Drag 37. Rheinzabern. The ovolo, *RF*.E40, and leaf P30 were shared by Attillus and Primitivus, but only Primitivus III seems to have arranged them like this: *LR* Taf 196, nos 7, 11, 12. Early–mid 3rd century.
Drag 33, Fig 22A, CG, Antonine; graffito SAEV on exterior between the girth groove and rim. The reading is 'SAEV' and is

probably part of a personal name, perhaps SAEVIUS in the genitive, so SAEV(II) (M Hassall, pers comm).

LD74 [186]
<SAM34>, Fig 18, (also LD74 [251.1]) Drag 37. Trier. In the style of the Primanus group. The ovolo, bear, hound, hare and rosette are on a signed bowl of Primanus and Dignus from London (Bird 1986, no. 2.87); the smaller dog is on Gard 1937, Taf 26, no. 9, and the leaf may be that on Taf 25, no. 14. *c* AD 235–50.
Drag 33, Fig 22B, EG, later 2nd–mid 3rd century.

LD74 [189]
<SAM66>, Fig 21, Drag 37. Rheinzabern. In the style of Pervincus, now numbered Pervincus I (Bittner 1986, 236, note 8). The ovolo has been almost totally removed, but his RF.E33 would fit; he also used the leaf P59 and arcade KB90. Cf *LR* Taf 238, no. 8. Second quarter 3rd century, probably. The band between rim and decoration is 40mm high.

LD74 [232]
Drag 38, Fig 22C, EG, later 2nd–mid 3rd century. Graffito on exterior.

LD74 [238]
<SAM77> Drag 41. Rheinzabern. With broad incision. Early–mid 3rd century.

LD74 [251.1]
<SAM9>, Fig 17, (also LD74 [F29]) Drag 37. Lezoux. Freestyle design, probably incorporating a sea-beast, dolphin and standing figure, but none is identifiable. Hadrianic–early Antonine.
<SAM45>, Fig 19, Drag 37. Rheinzabern. The ovolo, RF.E51, is recorded on 'Verschiedene Waren anschliessend an Reginus II, Julius I und Lupus'; the rosette may be O48, noted for the same style. Cf *LR* Taf 161, no. 15. First half 3rd century.

LD74 [289]
<SAM28>, Fig 18, Drag 37. Trier. The ovolo was shared by Dexter, Atillus and Dubitatus–Dubitus. Antonine–mid 3rd century; the fabric and finish suggest a date in the later part of the range.
<SAM32>, Fig 18, (also unphased LD74 [289.1]) Drag 37. Trier. In the style of Dubitatus–Dubitus. The decoration consists of beaded medallions containing a peacock on a column which is sometimes flanked by rings, alternating with fat columns supporting arcades over an owl perched on a leaf; between each of the main elements is a tree above a small coin-like roundel. The same arrangement is on Gard 1937, Taf 24, no. 4, and this bowl is likely to come from the same mould. *c* AD 225–45. The footring is heavy and square.
<SAM63>, Fig 21, Drag 37. Rheinzabern. In the style of Respectinus II, the only recorded user of the ovolo, RF.E37; the other motif is not identifiable. *c* AD 225–50.

LD74 [289.1]
<SAM36>, Fig 19, Drag 30. Rheinzabern. In the style of Cobnertus III. There is no apparent parallel for this small ovolo, but he seems to have been the sole user of the astragalus border, RF.O249; he also used the beadrow O264 and rosette O73, the archer M174, festoon KB85 and astragalus O197. The broken figure is not identifiable. *c* AD 160–90.

LD76 [32]
<SAM31>, Fig 18, Drag 37. Trier. The ovolo was used by Afer, Paternianus and Dubitatus. First half 3rd century. Very abraded.

LD76 [133]
<SAM68>, Fig 21, Drag 37. Rheinzabern. Ovolo RF.E23. The band between rim and decoration is 25mm high. Later 2nd–first half 3rd century.

LD76 [137]
<SAM76>, Fig 21, Drag 41. Rheinzabern. With incised palm branches (see <SAM75>) and a large rosette with dots at the tips of the petals. Early–mid 3rd century.

LD76 [210]
<SAM15>, Fig 17, Drag 37. Lezoux. The figure in the medallion is a cupid, *Oswald* 444A, used in a similar small medallion by Paternus II (*SS* pl 104, no. 8); the other figure may be similar to *Oswald* 545. Antonine.

LD76 [317]
<SAM6>, Fig 17, Drag 37. Montans. In the style of Chresimus or an associated potter. The ovolo and a similar wavy line border are shown on Simpson 1976, fig 5, nos 15, 17, and fig 6, nos 22–4, and the column on fig 4, no. 11. The triple festoon with spurred leaf is probably that on fig 6, no. 23. *c* AD 110–45.
<SAM48>, Fig 20, Drag 37. Rheinzabern. In the style of Verecundus II: for the ovolo RF.E10 and bead scroll KB95 with a plain scroll, cf *LR* Taf 173, nos 1, 2, 4. First half 3rd century. The band between rim and decoration is at least 55mm high.

LD76 [734]
<SAM17>, Fig 17, Drag 37. Lezoux. The lioness, *Oswald* 1569, was used by Cinnamus and Casurius; the fabric and poor impression suggest the latter (cf *SS* pl 137, no. 60). Mid to later Antonine.

LD74 [F17A]
<SAM11>, Fig 17, (also LD74 [F16], [F17B]) Drag 37. Lezoux. The ovolo, Rogers 1974, B85, was used by several potters, notably Cinnamus, whose motifs include rows of ovoid and astragalus beads. The caryatid, *Oswald* 1207A, is on a bowl in Cinnamus' style from the Beddingham villa, Sussex; the other figures are Diana, *Oswald* 117, a dolphin to right, *Oswald* 2384, and a dolphin to left (cf *Oswald* 2393). The ring terminals are unusual, and have perhaps been used to bridge the narrow space between festoon and border. *c* AD 145–75.
<SAM7>, Fig 17, Drag 37. Les Martres-de-Veyre. In the style of Cettus. The ovolo and tree are shown on *SS* pl 143, nos 34, 37. *c* AD 135–65.
<SAM16>, Fig 17, Drag 37. Lezoux. The figure is probably a panther, *Oswald* 1509. Antonine.
<SAM73>, Fig 21, (also LD74 [F17B]) Drag 30. Colchester. In the style of 'potter A'. The ovolo, rosette and wavy line border are on Hull 1963, fig 21, no. 1, the rosette and gladiators on fig 22, no. 3; fig 24, no. 10, has all the motifs in the same arrangement but with a line beneath the ovolo. Mid–later Antonine. The slip is almost completely lost.

LD74 [F17C]
<SAM8>, Fig 17, Drag 37. Lezoux. In the style of the Sacer–Attianus group. The Amazon, *Oswald* 241, is shown in a similar scroll on *SS* pl 83, no. 11; the leaf, circle, bird and astragalus are on pl 85, no. 6. *c* AD 125–50.

LD74 [F6]
<SAM69>, Fig 21, Drag 37. Rheinzabern. Ovolo RF.E26. Later 2nd–first half 3rd century.

LD74 [F18]
<SAM78> Large enclosed form (cf Oswald and Pryce 1920, pl 80, no. 3) with fragmentary incised foliage motifs. Rheinzabern. Later 2nd–first half 3rd century.

LD74 [F21]
<SAM39>, Fig 19, Drag 37. Rheinzabern. In the style of 'Kreis des Cerialis ware B': cf *LR* Taf 76, nos 10, 12, 14–18, for bowls in similar style, with the leafless tendrils, saltires, leaves, tree and ovolo. The individual motifs – ovolo RF.E39, leaves P84 and P99, tree P6, cupid M132, hare T163a and beadrow O258 – are all recorded for Cerialis. *c* AD 170–200. The band between rim and decoration is 70mm high.

LD74 [F29]
<SAM54>, Fig 20, Drag 37. Rheinzabern. In the style of Primitivus I, who used the acanthus, RF.P145, medallion K54 and beadrow O260; the motifs in the medallions are not identifiable. Early–mid 3rd century.

LD74 [F31]
<SAM14>, Fig 17, Drag 30 or Déch 68. Lezoux. With double medallion and foliage motif. There are no exact parallels for the leaf in Bémont 1977, but cf fig 42, no. 3. Antonine.

LD74 [1]
<SAM18>, Fig 17, Drag 37. Lezoux. Scroll with a large frilled leaf, probably a smaller version of Rogers 1974, H1. Similar small rings were used by Albucius (SS pl 122, no. 31) and Paternus II (pl 104, no. 10). The heavy scrollery and the finishing at the base suggest a mid–later Antonine date.

5.3 Samian potters' stamps

Brenda Dickinson

Introduction

Each entry gives the catalogue number, context, phase and land use (see Chapter 1.3–1.4). This is followed by the potter (i, ii, where homonyms are involved), die, form, reading, reference (if any), pottery of origin, discussion and date. Superscript (a) and (b) after pottery of origin indicate: (a) a stamp attested at the pottery in question and (b) assigned to the pottery on the evidence of fabric, distribution and so forth. Ligatured letters are underlined. All stamps are illustrated on Fig 23. The stamps are cross-referenced to the decorated and plain samian catalogue (5.2).

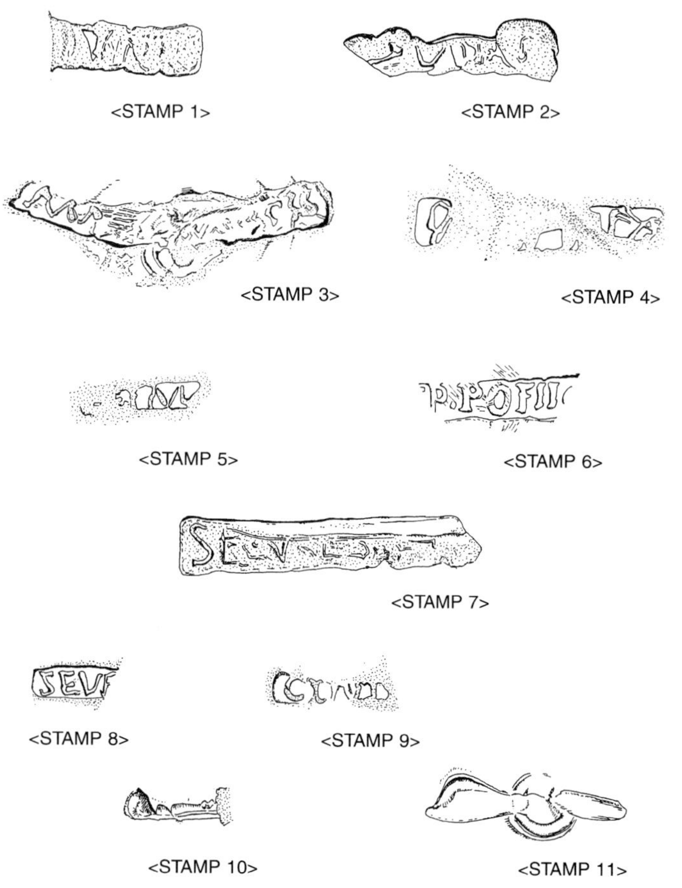

Fig 23 *Samian stamps <STAMP1>–<STAMP11> (scale 1:1)*

Catalogue

<STAMP7>, LD76 [710], phase2, OA2
Secundinus x? Avi... 2a Drag 37 mould-stamp (<SAM40>) SECVNDINI ΛVI (Ludowici 1927, 245) Rheinzabern[a]. It is not clear whether this stamp represents two potters, a Secundinus and an Avi(tus?), or one, named Secundinius Avi(tus?). At Rheinzabern it occurs in the decoration of a mould which has a stamp of Comitialis in the base and a signature (perhaps post cocturam) under the base (Ludowici and Ricken 1948, Taf. 78, 1F). The style of decoration associated with the stamp also has many details in common with Cerialis v's work. *c* AD175–220.

<STAMP3>, LD76 [358], phase 6, S4
Maianus iii 2d Drag 31R MLIAN VSF (Ludowici 1927, 220, d) Rheinzabern[a]. No clear example of the stamp has appeared yet, but Ludowici seems to suggest that the second A is barred. Maianus iii worked at both Ittenweiler and Rheinzabern, as is shown by the use of one of his dies at both potteries. Stamps from die 2d, however, are only so far attested at Rheinzabern. Like so many East Gaulish potters, he lacks site dating, but his use of some of the later East Gaulish forms at Rheinzabern, such as Drag 31R, Drag 32, Drag 39 and Lud Tb suggests a late 2nd- or early 3rd-century range. *c* AD 175–200.

<STAMP8>, LD76 [656], phase 6, S4
Severianus i 7a Drag 33 SEVE[RILNM] (Hartley 1969, fig 51, 14) Lezoux[a]. Severianus i is one of the potters represented, by a different stamp, in a group of late-Antonine samian recovered off Pudding Pan Rock, Kent. 7a is noted on forms Drag 31, Drag 31R, Drag 33 (including one from Pevensey) and Drag 38. He also stamped forms Wa 79, Wa 79R and Wa 80. *c* AD 160–220.

<STAMP2>, LD76 [700], phase 6, B1
Iulius viii 3f Drag 37 mould-stamp (<SAM58>) IVLIVS[E] retr. (Ludowici 1927, 242, a) Rheinzabern[a]. A decorated bowl with this stamp occurs in the later of two shipments of samian found at New Fresh Wharf, London (Bird 1986, 168, 2.115); the group is dated *c* AD 235–45 (ibid, 143). This evidence, and the style of the decoration on bowls with the same stamp, suggests a date in the second quarter of the 3rd century. *c* AD 225–50 (also unphased [22])

<STAMP10>, LD76 [252], phase 9, OA10
Illegible stamp Drag 31R East Gaulish. Rheinzabern ware, to judge by the fabric, and late 2nd century to early 3rd.

<STAMP4>, LD74 [4], phase 9, OA10
Pateriva 1a Drag 31 PATIIRIVL (V and L superimposed) (Frey 1993, Taf. XI, 221) Trier[b]. Although seven of the nine recorded examples of this stamp were found in Britain, where Trier ware is not particularly common, the fabrics and glazes suggest that they were made there. Of the other two, both in the Landesmuseum at Trier, one is probably from Trier and the other, from the Varuswald near Tholey, is in the right distribution area for Trier ware. Late 2nd century to early 3rd.

<STAMP6>, LD76 [281], unphased
Peppo 2a Drag 32 (?) [PII]P·POFII[C] (Ludowici 1927, 225, e) Rheinzabern[a]. Most of this potter's plain ware output consists of standard dishes of form Drag 32. Stamps from other dies have been noted from Hadrians' Wall (Chesters Museum, site not known), Malton and Osterburken. Later 2nd century to early 3rd.

<STAMP1>, LD74 [3], unphased
Comitialis 3a Drag 37 mould stamp (see <SAM41>) COMITILLISFC retr. (Ludowici 1927, 240, a) Rheinzabern[a]. Although this is one of the commonest mould-stamps found

on Rheinzabern decorated ware, there is no firm site dating for it. A stamp from a different die at Niederbieber and his decorative styles suggest a range *c* AD 175–220

<STAMP5>, LD74 [F17A], unphased
Paullus v 4a Drag 31 PAVLIM (Nash-Williams 1930, 178, 76) Lezoux[a]. Nearly all the stamps recorded from this die are on form Drag 31, but it was also used on forms Drag 31R, Drag 33 and Drag 38. Examples have been noted from Chesterholm and Chesters, both of which will be later than *c* AD 160. Stamps from another of Paullus v's dies occur in the late-Antonine plain ware from the Pudding Pan Rock wreck. *c* AD 160–200

<STAMP11>, LD74 [127], unphased
Illegible Drag 32 East Gaulish, Rheinzabern fabric. *c* AD 175–225.

<STAMP9>, LD74 [239], unphased
Drag 31 CIN[Central Gaulish, not paralleled by any other stamp in CIN[known to the present writer. Later 2nd century.

5.4 Glass

John Shepherd

Introduction

Ninety-two items of Roman glass, many just small splinters, were recovered from LD76. A single fragment of window glass was identified. The majority of the vessel glass fragments are from indeterminate forms in various metals. They are catalogued below according to metal colour. For each entry the catalogue number is given (eg <G1>) and the figure number where appropriate, followed by the accession number (in angled brackets), context number (in square brackets), phase and land use (eg S8). All finds are from LD76.

Vessel glass

Natural blue-green

<G1>
<689>, [296]; phase 7, S8
Small fragment from the rim of a small narrow-necked vessel. Free-blown; natural blue-green glass. Rim folded inwards and flattened out. 1st–3rd century.

<G2>
<690>, [258]; phase 9, OA10
As for <Gl>, natural blue-green glass.

<G3> (Fig 24)
<539>, [227]; phase 7, S8
Fragment from the rim of a small bowl or beaker. Free-blown; natural blue-green glass. Rim thickened, fire-rounded and slightly outsplayed. 1st–3rd century.

<G4> (Fig 24)
<705>, [365]; phase 6, S4
Fragment from the rim and side of a bowl. Free-blown, natural blue-green glass. Rim thickened, fire-rounded and outsplayed. 1st–3rd century.

<G5>
<552>, [327]; phase 6, S4
Small fragment from the neck of a bottle (Isings 1957, 63–9, form 50/51). Free-blown; thick natural blue-green glass. Late 1st or 2nd century.

<G6>–<G16>
<547>, [255], <556>, [256]; phase 7, OA8; <688>, [240], <696>, [290]; phase 7, S8; <543>, [310]; phase 6, B1; <563>, [357], <786>, [363], <558>, [366], <554>, [640]; phase 6, S4; <702>, [523]; residual
Eleven fragments of thick (*c* 1.5–2.0mm) natural blue-green glass from an indeterminate number of free-blown vessels.

<G17>–<G29>
<562>, [274], <533>, [279], <560>, [527], <557>, [659]; phase 6, S4; <550>, [228], <695>, [290]; phase 7, S8; <712>, [144], residual
Thirteen fragments of thin natural blue-green glass from an indeterminate number of free-blown vessels.

Poor, colourless and greenish-colourless glass

No fragments of the distinctive late Roman greenish-colourless metals were found. All the fragments below represent metals which were probably intended to be 'colourless' but retain a faint greenish tint.

<G30>(Fig 24)
<681>, [361]; phase 6, S4
Part of the shoulder and part of the neck of a small bulbous flask (Isings 1957, 122–5, form 104 a or b; see below for a discussion of this vessel). Free-blown; colourless glass with a greenish tint. Neck tapers slightly outwards towards the lip of the vessel of which nothing survives. Body decorated with pairs of horizontal wheel-cut lines of which just two pairs are extant. Mid 3rd or 4th century.

<G31>
<540>, [200]; phase 7, S8
Fragment from the side of a beaker or flask. Free-blown; colourless glass. Decorated with four horizontal wheel-cut lines. Late 2nd–4th century.

<G32>
<694>, [146]; phase 6, S4
Fragment from the handle of a flask or bottle. Free-blown vessel; thick greenish-colourless glass distorted by contact with fire. Applied handle with an oval flattened 'spur'. 3rd or 4th century.

G<33> (Fig 24)
<545>, [640]; phase 6, S4
Fragment from the rim and side of a beaker or bowl (possibly an 'Airlie' type bowl – Isings 1957, 102–3, form 85b). Free-blown; thick colourless glass. Rim thickened, fire-rounded and sloping slightly inwards. Late 2nd or 3rd century.

<G34> (Fig 24)
<542>, [354]; phase 5, OA5
Fragment from the rim and side of a hemispherical cup, Free-blown; thick greenish-colourless glass. Rim thickened, fire-rounded and outsplayed. 3rd or 4th century.

<G35> (Fig 24)
<540>, [200]; phase 7, S8
Fragment from the rim and side of a bowl or beaker. Free-blown; thick colourless glass with a greenish tint. Rim thickened, fire-rounded and slightly outsplayed. 3rd or 4th century.

G<36>–<G62> (Fig 24)
<541>–<561>, [261]; phase 6, S4
Twenty-seven fragments, only a few of which join together, from the side and lower part of an 'indented' bowl (Isings 1957, 147–8, form 117). Free-blown; thick colourless glass with a greenish tint. Decorated with large, vertically orientated, oval indentations of which just two are extant (originally five or six). Late 3rd or 4th century.

G<63> (Fig 24)
<544>, [228]; phase 7, S8
Fragment from the side of a bowl or beaker. Free-blown; colourless glass with a greenish tint. Decorated with applied and marvered relief prunts, just one of which is extant. 3rd or 4th century.

<G64> (Fig 24)
<679>, [341]; phase 5, OA5
Fragment from the base of a small beaker. Free-blown; greenish colourless glass. Flattened base, thickened and cut out. 3rd or 4th century.

<G65>
<546>, [438], not allocated
Small fragment from the base of a bowl or beaker. Free-blown; colourless with a greenish tint. Applied solid base ring. 3rd or 4th century.

<G73>
<691> [239], <549>, [252]; phase 9, OA10; <698>, [303]; phase 7, S8; <699>, [306]; phase 2, OA2; <559>, [659], <564>, [674]; phase 6, B1
Eight fragments of thick (*c* 1.5–2.0mm) colourless glass with a greenish tint from an indeterminate number of free-blown vessels.

<G74>–<G82>
<540>, [200], <680>, [290]; phase 7, S8; <555>, [256]; phase 7, OA8; <543>, [310]; phase 6, B1; <557>, [659]; phase 6, S4
Nine fragments of thin colourless glass with a faint greenish tint from an indeterminate number of free-blown vessels.

<G84>
<547>, [255]; phase 7, OA8; <680>, [290]; phase 7, S8
Two fragments of thick (*c*1.5–2.0mm) greenish-colourless glass from an indeterminate number of free-blown vessels.

G<85>–<G91>
<550>, [228]; phase 7, S8; <000>, [267], residual
Seven fragments of thin greenish-colourless glass from an indeterminate number of free-blown vessels.

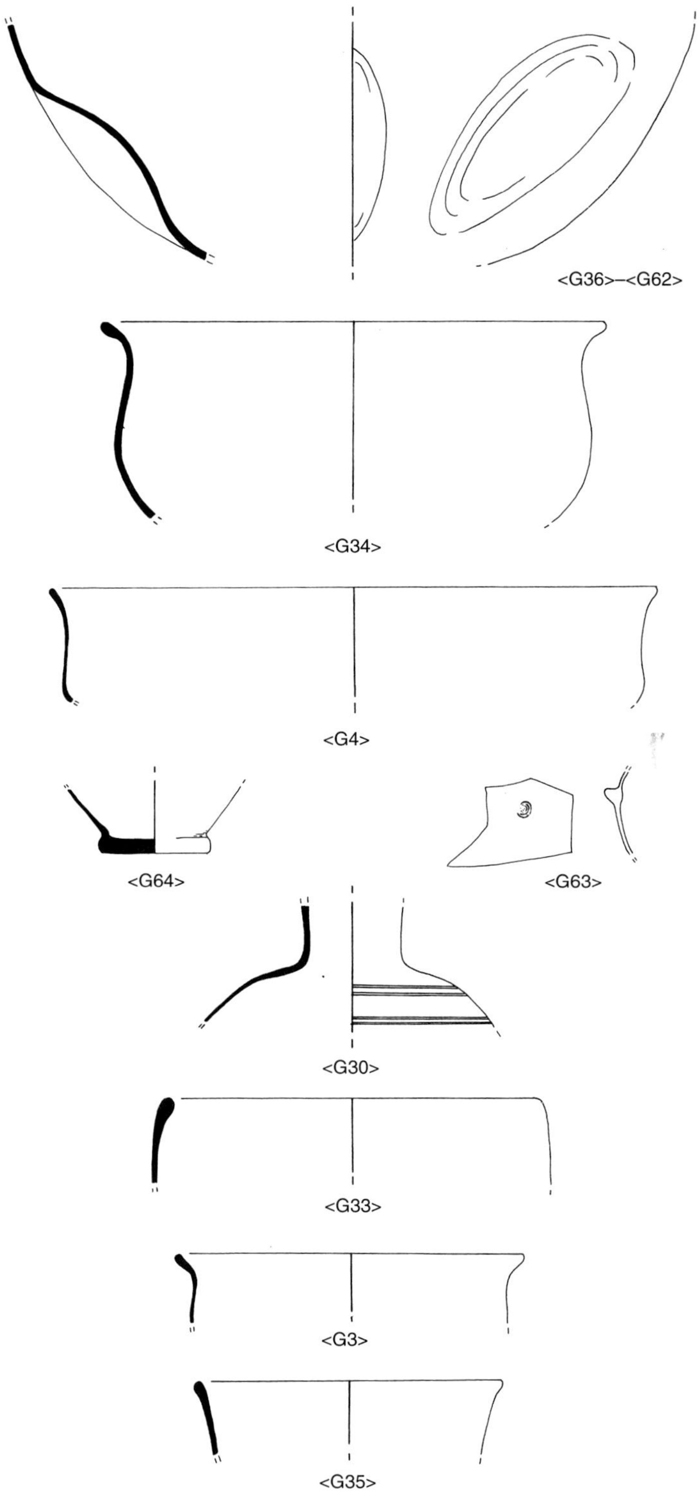

Fig 24 *Glass vessels (scale 1:2)*

Discussion

In general, this assemblage is too small and too fragmentary to make any detailed comments about the supply of glass to this site. Some fragments of 1st- or 2nd-century vessels are represented here, for example the common bottle <G5> and some, perhaps all, of the fragments <G6>–<G29> on account of their colour. However, these are particularly small and some show signs of heavy abrasion, suggesting that they might well be residual material. The greater part of the assemblage, in particular the colourless and greenish-colourless glass, dates to the 3rd and 4th centuries but again there is an important point to notice. There is an absence of the distinctive and well-known metals and forms characteristic of the 4th century, for example greenish-colourless metals, often poorly made with many air bubbles and solid inclusions; bowls and conical beakers with simple rim and base forms, especially the knocked-off, rough rim (see Price 1979 for an analysis with many discussions of typical 4th-century metals and forms in relation to those from Frocester Court, Glos). It might be, therefore, that the majority of the 'later' glass from this site pre-dates the time when such forms and metals were in use.

Leaving aside the majority of the fragments, which represent flasks, bowls and beakers for which insufficient has survived to allow for a more detailed identification, only two vessels deserve additional comment. These two vessels, from a ditch (S4) in phase 6 (the bulbous flask <G30>, Fig 24; and the indented bowl <G36>–<G62>, Fig 24) are not uncommon in late Roman assemblages, but the fact that so much of such thin-bodied vessels has survived is surprising. It is possible that their survival nearly complete indicates that that is how they were when originally deposited.

A precise identification of the form of the flask <G30> is not possible since only the shoulder and part of the neck survive. The absence of a constriction at the junction of the neck of the flask with its body, it being cylindrical and flaring slightly towards the lip, would suggest that it belongs to Isings form 104 (rather than her form 103 with constricted neck that tapers inwards towards the lip). Without any base fragments it is not possible to assign it to one of her sub-categories (Isings form 104a with base ring, form 104b without). The form in general, however, has been well-discussed by Harden with respect to an example with a simple concave base ('the ordinary flask', Isings 1957, 123–4, form 104b) from a grave in the Minories, Aldgate (Harden and Green 1978, 163–76).

Its production appears to have begun during the 3rd century but they are more prolific during the 4th (Harden gives numerous references to continental examples but can cite only two British finds, namely Chilgrove, Sussex, and Baldock, Herts). He notes that the metal of the Minories example, being good colourless glass, probably pre-dates the use of the poorer greenish-colourless glass used for such vessels (and other forms) in the 4th century and so assigns it to the beginning of the form's production, that is mid to late 3rd century. This observation is of particular interest here since the Shadwell example is in a similar metal and his interpretation mirrors the general comments made above about this assemblage as a whole.

The same is also true for the 'indented' bowl <G36>–<G62> since it too is more commonly found among 4th-century assemblages (Isings 1957, 147–8, form 117) but, like the flask, it is made in a good, colourless metal. All datable examples of this form belong to the 4th century (for example, Namur, Andernach, Mayen, Koln, Nymegen: see Isings 1957, 147f) but one, from Strasbourg, is late 3rd or 4th century. The metal and associations of this Shadwell example, however, might suggest that its production should be pushed back into the 3rd or, at least, very early 4th century.

Of the remaining vessels, all have fire-rounded rims which, though found elsewhere contemporary with the coarse knocked-off and rough rims (Price 1979, 43) of the 4th century, are not as common then as they are in the previous century. They are represented here in good metals which, once again, are not entirely compatible with 4th-century repertoires.

One vessel, however, is certainly earlier than most. The bowl rim <G33> is similar to those of the 'Airlie' type bowl (Isings 1957, 102, form 85b) which are datable from the end of the 2nd to the middle of the 3rd century. They are common among assemblages of that date and probably represent the standard drinking form of that period. Whether it is directly associated with the bulbous flask and the indented bowl discussed above (they are all in similar metals) or whether it belongs to the handful of residual fragments is impossible to resolve.

5.5 Accessioned finds

Angela Wardle

Introduction

Roman artefacts were found at both LD74 and LD76, but many of the objects which were undoubtedly retrieved in 1974 can no longer be traced. The surviving finds have been recorded in accordance with current MoL standards and are held in the archive. Nearly seven hundred of the thousand items recovered are of Roman date, the vast majority of these being coins, with nearly one hundred fragments of Roman glass vessels. The catalogue is arranged according to function and the stratigraphic context given wherever possible. For each entry the catalogue number (in angled brackets) is given and the figure number where appropriate, followed by the accession number (in angled brackets), context number (in square brackets), phase and land use. General discussion of the assemblage has been incorporated within the main text.

Finds are from LD76, except where stated otherwise. In addition to conventions used throughout (see 1.3, 1.4) the following abbreviations have been used:L (length); W (width); H (height); Diam (diameter).

Personal ornament and dress accessories

Brooches

<S1> (Fig 25)
<241> [657]; phase 6, S4
Incomplete; Diam 28mm. Copper alloy plate brooch decorated with cloisonné enamelling in three zones arranged in concentric circles around the centre. The enamel in the central roundel is lost; it is encircled by a zone of red enamel set with at least sixteen contrasting dots in ?green. The outer band is dark blue and is surrounded by a copper alloy border which has not survived well. There are traces of a sprung pin mechanism on the back. 2nd century.

<S2>
<290>, [23]; phase 10, OA11
Copper alloy. Fragment of catchplate; type of brooch unknown, but it probably dates from the 1st or 2nd century.

Finger ring

<S3> (Fig 25)
<219>, [144]; unphased
Diam 18mm; internal Diam 15.5mm. Copper alloy finger ring with eight faces on the exterior of the hoop, and plain circular interior. It is a well-known 3rd-century form (Henig 1978, 35, fig 1, IX), and others are known from London, as for example an inscribed ring from Rangoon Street (RAG82, 1351–127).

Hairpins

<S4> (Fig 25)
<50>, [273]; phase 10, OA11
Incomplete; L 38mm; W of head 8.5mm. The upper part of a jet hairpin with faceted cube head and swelling shank, broken at about the mid point. This is the most common type of jet pin seen at York (Allason-Jones 1996, 40) and is frequently found as a hair ornament in later Roman burials.

<S5> (Fig 25)
<279>, [268]; phase 7, OA8
Incomplete; L 46mm. Bone pin, Crummy type 3 (Crummy 1983, 21), with spherical head, dating after AD 150.

<S6> (Fig 25)
<253>, [72]; phase 7, OA8
Incomplete; surviving L 33.5mm. Bone pin, Crummy type 3, with globular head, as above.

The following are all incomplete fragments of bone pin shaft and it has not been possible to ascribe them to a type.

<S7>, <284>, [361]; phase 6, S4

<S8>, <769>, [290]; phase 7, S8

<S9>, <283>, [228]; phase 7, S8

<S10>, <384>, [356]; phase 6, S4

<S11>, <381>, [366]; phase 6, S4

<S12>, <281>, [1274]; phase 9 OA10

<S13>, <270>, [23]; phase 10, OA11

Bracelets

<S14> (Fig 25)
<91>, [0]; unstratified
Object not located; described from drawing.
Fragment of copper alloy strip

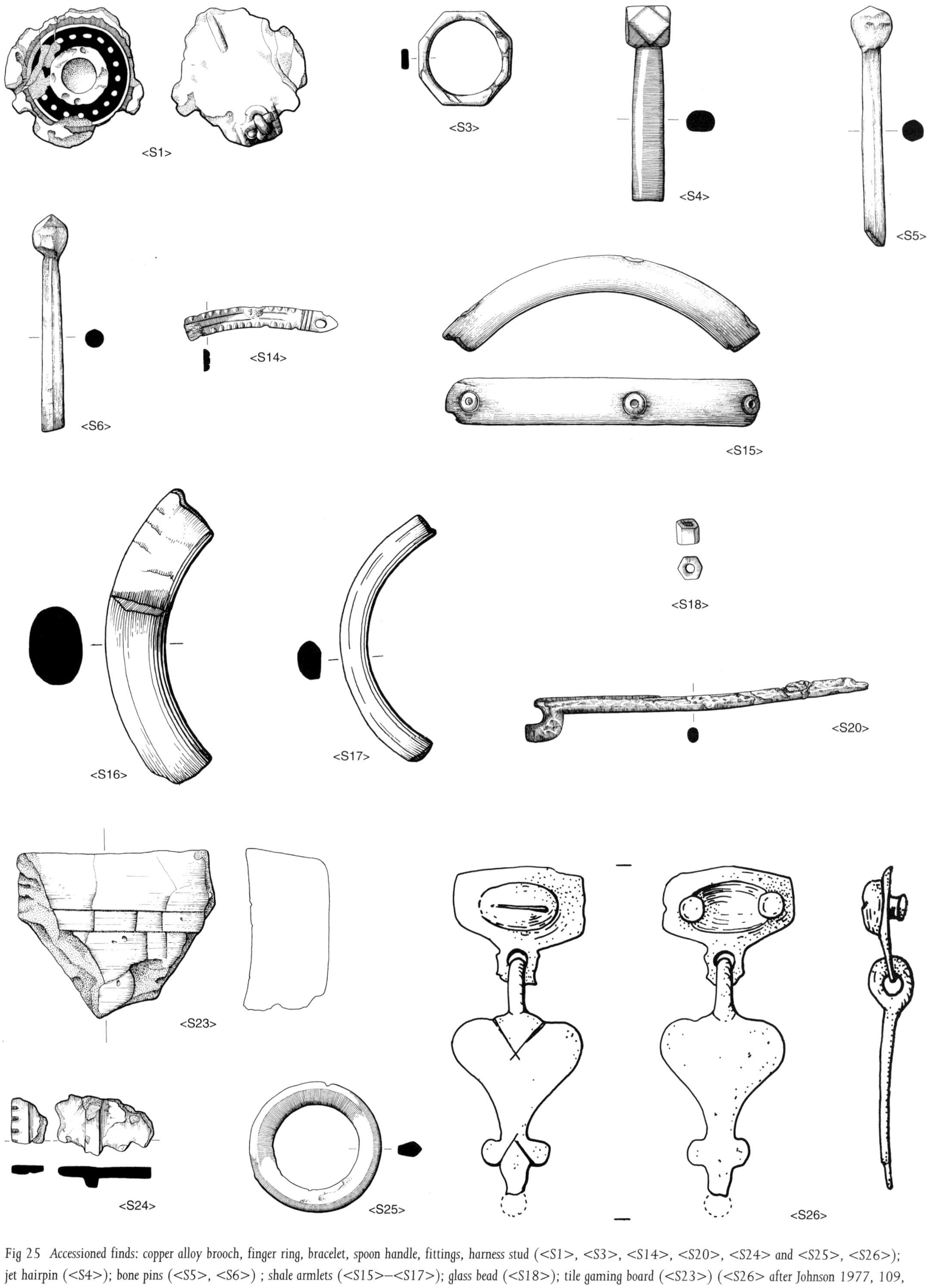

Fig 25 *Accessioned finds: copper alloy brooch, finger ring, bracelet, spoon handle, fittings, harness stud (<S1>, <S3>, <S14>, <S20>, <S24> and <S25>, <S26>); jet hairpin (<S4>); bone pins (<S5>, <S6>) ; shale armlets (<S15>–<S17>); glass bead (<S18>); tile gaming board (<S23>) (<S26> after Johnson 1977, 109, fig 39) (scale 1:1, except <S23> 1:2)*

bracelet; L 29mm; W 4mm; engraved linear decoration along the centre of the band and V-shaped notches along the edges; rounded terminal pierced with a circular hole for a catch. 3rd/4th century.

<S15> (Fig 25)
<272>, [1274]; phase 9, OA10
Fragment of shale armlet with oval cross section, W 8.5mm. The outer face is decorated with a series of neatly-cut dot and circle motifs. Approximate Diam 75mm.

<S16> (Fig 25)
<258>, [23]; phase 10, OA11
Incomplete, fragment of plain shale armlet with oval cross-section, W15mm. Approximate Diam 80mm.

<S17> (Fig 25)
<258>, [23]; phase 10, OA11
Incomplete, fragment of plain shale armlet with oval cross-section, W 7mm. Approximate Diam 40mm, possibly for use by a child. The inside of the bangle shows the V-shaped section formed when the circle was cut from the parent disc (Lawson 1975, 242). Allason-Jones (1996, 35) suggests that small rings, which often retain their turning scars, could have an alternative function, perhaps as belt dividers. Their presence in graves at York might also suggest that they were used for ritual purposes (ibid). Hair rings, which are also known, are usually of smaller diameter, up to 20mm (ibid 46, no. 283).

Bead

<S18> (Fig 25)
<241>, [146]; phase 6, S4
Object not located, described from original records. Complete; L 5mm. Green glass bead, six sided, imitating an emerald crystal.

Toilet implement

<S19>
<210>, [23]; phase 10, OA11
Incomplete; L 20mm. Copper alloy tweezers. The spring and part of the arms of a pair of plain tweezers, made from a single strip of metal.

Spoon

<S20> (Fig 25)
<269>, [228]; phase 7, S8
Incomplete; L 67mm. Copper alloy spoon. Part of the handle and 'goose neck' junction of the handle with the lower spoon bowl.

Ceramic lamps

<S21> (Fig 13)
LD74 <2>, LD74 [1]; phase 9, OA10
Complete; L 90.5mm; W 48.5mm; H 27mm. *Firmalampe* of Loeschcke type X, with closed nozzle channel. There are two vestigial lugs on the shoulder; integral ring handle. Plain base.

<S22> (Fig 13)
LD74 <3>, LD74 [1]; phase 9, OA10
Complete; L 101.5mm; W 57.5mm; H 25.5mm. *Firmalampe* of Loeschcke type IX, the nozzle channel open at the discus end. Two vestigial, but sharply moulded, lugs on the shoulder and an integral ring handle. Shallow moulded foot ring on base.

Gaming board

<S23> (Fig 25)
<305>, [1080]; phase 9, OA10
Object not located; described from original drawing. Fragment of tile 76 x 64mm, on which are inscribed two parallel lines, with others at right angles to them, creating an irregular chequer board effect. Although irregular, these could be the markings for an impromptu gaming board, for which there are many parallels.

Fittings

<S24> (Fig 25)
<271>, [255]; phase 7, OA8
Incomplete; L 19mm. Fragment of cast copper alloy with a central rib on the back and traces of cut-out decoration on one edge; all edges are broken. This could be from a mount, possibly a harness mount, or part of an attachment for a copper alloy vessel.

<S25> (Fig 25)
<265>, [666]; phase 6, S4
Complete; Diam external 25mm; internal 17mm. Copper alloy ring fitting with faceted section.

Military equipment

<S26> (Fig 25)
context uncertain
This object is only known from an archive drawing and was possibly found during trial trenching on the site which was later to be LD76. Almost complete; L 65mm overall; W of stud 26mm. Copper alloy. Vulvate strap mount with suspension loop from which hangs a bi-lobed pendant. The stud is clearly a leather fitting, as can be seen by the fungiform studs on the reverse and it is of a type that is found during the latter part of the 2nd and 3rd century, frequently in military contexts (Bishop 1996, 71, no. 440 from Aldborough). There are further continental parallels from such sites as Nijmegen (Zadoks-Josephus Jitta et al 1973, 30 no. 73) and the Saalburg (Bishop and Coulston 1993, 156 no. 14).

Industrial material

<S27>
[1277]; phase 9, OA10
Ceramic mould for the casting of a copper alloy object. The find cannot now be located and the following is taken from an archive note by Sarnia Butcher, dated February 1978. 'Very little of the object to be cast can be seen in the part of the mould preserved, but it appears to be a disc of approximately 30mm diam, with a decorated rim and signs of a stepped centre. This might be part of a plate brooch, or decorative mount or stud. There are some unusual details; the border design, of repeated chevrons, would be cast in relief rather than, as on most Roman provincial trinkets, being engraved in the surface of the object itself. The small round lugs lie close to the rim of the disc but do not actually join it. Some Roman provincial disc-brooches have lugs round the rim but these are more regularly spaced and no example is known to the writer which has a raised centre; there is usually a recessed design or a cell to hold enamel. This might suggest that these lugs are intended for the registration parts of the mould.'

5.6 Roman coins

Michael Hammerson

Introduction

A total of 474 Roman coins were recovered from the excavations which is high for sites of this size and limited stratification. Although 42% (199) were from levels deemed to be post-Roman, or unphased, it has been assumed in this report that they too derive from the Roman occupation of the site. A detailed list of the coins is available in the archive held by the LAARC.

Discussion

The overall totals

In interpreting the relative numbers of coins from the various phases of occupation on a Roman site, it is necessary to be aware of the political, military and social influences exerted by, and on the production of, that unique commodity, money, and the pitfalls into which uninformed interpretation can lead. The production of coinage varied dramatically throughout the Roman era, as did its supply to different parts of the empire and the length of circulation of any particular coin type. The relative values of coins of different periods differed greatly, rendering comparison of some periods – often close in time – very difficult. The length of each period in the histogram (Fig 26) is not consistent, some relating to a reign, and others to a recognised numismatic period based on the use of a particular type of coin. Further, the strait-jacketing of coins of one period into a histogram bar masks the fact that those coins would normally have seen circulation well past their period of issue, and may not even have reached the site until long after that time. Finally, numbers may often be affected by the chance survival or destruction of archaeological levels, particularly the later, uppermost ones. Given all these cautions, however, a consistency among different types of sites does emerge, when coins survive in sufficient numbers for a pattern to be discerned.

In overall terms, looking at the whole period of Roman occupation, the histogram bears little or no resemblance to those of the major settlements in the region. Those for Southwark and Staines (Hammerson 1996, 161) show very different patterns of coinage over the Roman period. It is regrettable that there is not, as yet, any comprehensive assessment of the Roman coinage from the city of London. It would be incautious to take existing histograms (eg Hammerson 1978) and from recent sites (eg Guildhall Yard, Hammerson 1997) as representative of the overall city coinage; the dangers of this approach are shown in Hammerson 1996, 160–4. However, the same study shows a considerably closer resemblance to the histograms for three 'satellite' settlements of Londinium: Brentford, Enfield and the relatively-close Old Ford (Fig 2; Hammerson 1996, 161). While the nature of these settlements is not as yet fully understood, the finding of quantities of butchered animal bone at Old Ford suggests that one function of these sites, as the last stop along the road to Londinium, may have been that of a market, a suggestion perhaps reinforced by the relatively high quantities of coinage (notably of the later Roman period) found there.

At Brentford, Old Ford, Enfield and Shadwell the low numbers of 1st- and 2nd-century coinage suggest little activity during that period. However, coinage from that period is relatively scarce on rural sites; the coinage itself is large, with an intrinsically high value, and more likely to be carefully sought if dropped; and the other three sites have yielded other finds, such as pottery, from the earlier periods. The coins from Enfield, in particular, and to a lesser extent Brentford, suggest a reasonable level of activity during the 1st and 2nd centuries. The presence of several burials on this site, and the possible reinterpretation of Structure 1, as a mausoleum, or the *cella* of a temple, perhaps associated with the cemetery, remind us that an alternative explanation may lie in any or all of the coins representing votive or other religious offerings.

The sudden leap in coin numbers after the 250s is a common phenomenon on what may be termed 'normal' Roman sites (Hammerson 1996, 155). The 152 'official' coins of AD 259–73, and the 124 irregular coins from *c* AD 270–85, may not represent such a differential, in terms of purchasing power, over the four better base-silver coins of AD 238–53, as might appear at first sight (Fig 26). A similarly misleading picture is commonly found on sites, including Shadwell, for the period AD 296–310; this was the era of Diocletian's major reform of the coinage, when all previous coins were replaced by large, good quality folles; these occur in quantity in British hoards but are rarely found as casual losses on sites. Anomalously, the absence of coins on the histogram bar for AD 296–310 may actually represent a period of stability, relative prosperity and low inflation. The period also follows the suppression of the revolt of Carausius and Allectus (AD 287–96), and the political situation in Britain in the following years may have brought less benevolent results; for example, Diocletian closed the London Mint in AD 296, it was not reopened for some two decades, and was permanently closed in AD325–6.

All of the 1st- and 2nd-century coins show medium to very heavy wear, indicating that none need have found their way to the site prior to the later years of the 1st century, and these coins circulated, in worn condition, into the 260s. The coin evidence, therefore, would not be inconsistent with the construction of the 'tower', at some time between AD 150/175 and AD 250; indeed, some form of activity on the site during the 250s is suggested by the three coins of Maximinus I, Trebonianus Gallus and Volusian, all uncommon as British site finds, the first showing some wear, and the others only slight wear.

Selected Roman coinage

The presence of a Durotrigian Stater of the late 1st century BC (LD74 <35>) is unexpected. The distribution map (in Mack 1975, 118) indicates that few Durotrigian coins have been found beyond the immediate tribal area of Dorset, Wiltshire and, to a lesser extent, Somerset, and even fewer in or beyond the London region. Though in theory demonetised following the introduction of Roman coinage at the time of the Conquest, hoard and stratified finds suggest that Iron Age coins saw limited use, on an unknown basis, until perhaps the later 1st century. The context in which this coin was found dated to the 4th century and therefore it is residual.

From another late Roman context came a worn as or dupondius of Hadrian (LD74 <326>), clipped down to 21mm in diameter. This 1st- and 2nd-century smaller bronze coinage certainly saw circulation until the later years of the 2nd century, though the great majority of earlier bronze coins from 3rd-century contexts, especially hoards, are the larger sestertii. They are rarely found clipped down, certainly during the period in which they circulated; one possibility, therefore, is that this example may have circulated until the 270s, and been clipped down for metal to produce irregular antoniniani. However, it would presumably, by this time, have been demonetised itself, rendering it valueless, except possibly in the eyes of someone who hoped it might, even clipped, retain some value, and some other explanation may be necessary.

Two copper alloy copies of Severan denarii were found, coated with a silver wash to make them look like genuine coins (LD76 <266>, LD74 <374>). Whilst these imitation coins are common, they mimic official issues which were themselves debased in the 190s. They were clearly produced from casts of official coins and, unlike the coins from most of the other Romano-British phases of coin imitation, which are considered to have at least had official sanction, these early 3rd-century copies (which also imitate denarii of earlier emperors) are probably deliberate forgeries, produced illegally and intended to deceive.

Of individual note are the two coins of Tacitus (AD 275–6; LD74 <58> and <322>), both from mid to later 4th-century contexts, since they would probably have gone out of circulation by the 280s or 290s. Coins of this short-lived emperor are rare as either site or hoard finds, and the presence of two examples here as site finds is of some interest. Together with the two coins of Aurelian (LD74 <61> and <161>), and the single one of Probus (LD74 <397>), also from post-mid 4th-century levels, which are also scarce as site finds, the presence of these reformed post-270 antoniniani provides an interesting – if not readily interpretable – numismatic transition on the site, between the regular and irregular antoniniani of the period AD 259–85, and the issues of AD 287–96.

Though not uncommon in themselves, the proportion of the total site coinage represented by issues of the rebel British emperors Carausius (AD 287–93) and Allectus (AD 293–6), varies considerably between sites, and is not predictable as part of any pattern. On some sites or settlements, including most of those London region sites commented upon above, they are rare or scarce. However, their presence at Shadwell, in numbers sufficient to make them the third most numerous numismatic period, is perhaps one of this site's most distinguishing features, with 28 of Carausius and 11 of Allectus. Indeed, their presence in such relatively high numbers may have been a factor leading to the original interpretation of the site as a signal station, by suggesting a contemporaneity of activity with the earlier phases of the Saxon Shore system, and particularly with Carausius's use of it as a defence against the central Roman powers.

All of the coins from this period derive from contexts not earlier than the mid 4th century. Since these coins would undoubtedly have been withdrawn from circulation after Diocletian's recovery of the province, they presumably derive from disturbed late 3rd-century levels; certainly period 4, phase 8, from which the highest proportion of these coins was recovered, contained large quantities of residual 3rd-century material.

Three Carausian coins (all were antoniniani) are of individual interest.

LD74 <350>
obv: VIRTVS CARAVSI AVG, Cuirassed bust l, with spear
rev: PAX AVG, mint mark S P over MLXXI, type not recorded in *Roman imperial coinage* (*RIC*) (Mattingly et al 1923–94).

LD76 <78>
obv: IMP C CARAVSIVS AVG, bust l
rev: MONETA AVGGG, mint mark S P over MC, type not recorded in *RIC* (ibid).

LD74 <721>
Scarce Legionary type as *RIC* 58 or 89 (LEG II AVG), or *RIC* 801 (LEG IIXX PRIMIG) (ibid).

LD74 <429>, a coin of AD 321, is something of an enigma. Though the phase of imitations of the 340s (see below) copied all of the types in circulation at the time, it is likely that the coins of pre-330 had been withdrawn by the reform of that year. Nevertheless, coins clearly imitating those of the 320s are found, albeit rarely, but they are usually of the poorer quality, as regards competence of engraving and production, and size, commonly (though not invariably) found among the 340s copies. This example would have been identified as a full-sized official issue of the familiar BEATA TRANQVILLITAS issues of the time, were it not for the name in the obverse legend, which reads CONNTANTINVS rather than CONSTANTINVS. Is it, therefore, an unusually good quality 340s imitation, or an official coin of 321 incorporating a genuine engraver's error which escaped notice at the mint?

The coin patterns from the majority of Romano-British 4th-century sites fall into a limited number of similar but distinctive patterns, which suggest a degree of uniformity of economic and other conditions across much of the province, reflecting, on the whole, a settled central control, at least until the 360s, after which the main differences occur. As seen above, site finds of coins from AD 296–310, the period of Diocletian's large reformed folles, are usually very few (though hoards indicate their presence in some numbers); the Shadwell figure (nil) decisively reflects this. During the 310s and 320s, a gradual reduction in the module of the coins – presumably a sign of returning inflation – sees a general increase in the numbers of site finds, which is accentuated during the more drastic reforms of AD 330 and AD 341, and the apparent cessation of coin production at the western mints between *c* AD 340 and 350 (perhaps AD 341–6). This caused two further phases of officially-sanctioned copying of the coinage, the first during the 340s (Hammerson 1980) and the second between *c* AD 355 and 365 (the 'fallen horseman' imitations), in both of which phases the coins were often produced in very large quantities. Many of them are so small and crude that the designs they imitate are barely recognisable.

As at Old Ford, Enfield and Brentford and, indeed, Southwark, the Shadwell histogram (Fig 26) shows a minor peak in the 340s. They similarly show a more unusual falling-off in numbers during the 350s–360s 'fallen horseman imitations' period, when numbers are often immensely common on some sites. Numbers then show a small 'recovery' during the Valentinianic period, differing from Staines, which is one of those sites where numbers fall off from the mid 350s, never to recover.

All these sites show few or no coins of the period AD 378–88. Then they divide into one of two categories: one which continues its numismatic 'decline' to the end of the Roman period, the other which shows a final increase in numbers in the Theodosian period (AD 388–402), after which Roman coinage effectively ceases to find its way to Britain (perhaps the best-known example of this is Richborough, Kent, where very large numbers of Theodosian issues occur). Southwark, Brentford and Enfield tend towards the former category, while Shadwell shows it to a marked extent, with no coins later than AD 388. Conversely, Staines and Old Ford show the latter pattern (though only at Old Ford are the numbers significant enough to be useful).

Therefore, on the basis of the coinage, and particularly the latest coin, of Flavius Victor (AD 387–8), activity (or, at least, use of coins) at Shadwell ceases by *c* AD 390 or not long after. However, the silver siliqua of Magnus Maximus (AD 270–365) (LD74 <101>), from an unphased context, represents a coin with some purchasing power, though speculation on the reason for its presence would be unprofitable.

Roman coins by period and phase

Table 14 examines whether any information can be derived from a study of the coins from the site according to the chronology of the periods and phases from which they were recovered.

Of the phases which yielded coins, only one (phase 2) is dated to the 1st century, This is in itself associated with a build-up of later levels, and the only two coins from it are from the third quarter of the 3rd century. The only coin from phase 4 is of a similar date, though this accords exactly with the dating for the phase.

Phases 5, 6 and 7 all date generally to the later 3rd century, with some overlap into the 4th century. Twenty-seven of the 40 coins from it are from the period AD 253–85; deficiencies in the site records might account for the later examples, though the three worn examples of 1st- to 2nd-century coins could conceivably have seen use into the 260s or 270s AD and are not necessarily out of place here; the Severan coin, by contrast, is most likely residual.

Of the 251 coins from phases 8, 9 and 10 (all mid to late 4th century), 207 were closely datable and 95% of those dated to AD 253 or later. The 3rd-century (and earlier) coins would almost certainly be predominantly residual in these contexts (though hoard evidence does suggest that the occasional antoninianus was made some use of in the 4th century), leaving 33 coins from the 4th century, and perhaps no more than ten which would have seen circulation in the post-AD 360 period. Residuality is clearly a factor here.

The unstratified coins appear, in general, to reflect the frequency of their stratified counterparts. There is, further, the reasonably encouraging factor that the later the coins, the more likely they are to occur in residual contexts. Of the AD 340s coins, 45% (9 out of 20) are residual, of the issues of AD 350–65, 66% (8 out of 12), of the Valentinianic issues, 77% (14 out of 18), and 100% of the three post-AD 378 coins.

In general, then, although the stratigraphy of the site is not perhaps clear enough to enable such a table to permit close dating of the predominantly later Roman contexts, the virtual

	Phased contexts								Unphased contexts	
	Period 2	Period 3			Periods 4 and 5				LD74	LD76
Coin date	Phase 2	Phase 4	Phase 5	Phase 6	Phase 7	Phase 8	Phase 9	Phase 10		
Iron Age							1			
1st century AD			1	1						
98–138							1		1	1
138–61						1	1	1	4	1
161–80					1		2		1	
180–92									1	
2nd century									2	
192–213				1				1	3	
222–53						1	1		1	1
1st half 3rd century						1			1	
253–73 (regular)	1	1	1	1	5	26	34	9	51	18
270–82 (regular)						3	1			
c 270–85 (irregular)	1		2	2	19	27	26	8	25	17
287–96						21	5	3	8	2
310–20						1	2	2	4	1
320–30				1		4			1	1
330–41				1	1	3	1	2	5	
347–50 (regular)						1		1	2	2
c 340–50 (irregular)					3	2	4	2	7	2
351–5						3			1	1
c 355–65							1		5	1
364–78						1	1	2*	9	5
378–83									1	
383–8									2	
Illegible *c* 270–365					1	5	10	2	11	
Illegible					3	19	3	5**		

* Includes 15th-century French jetton
** Includes one 1614–25 and one of possibly 18th-century date

Table 14 Summary of Roman coins by phase and coin date

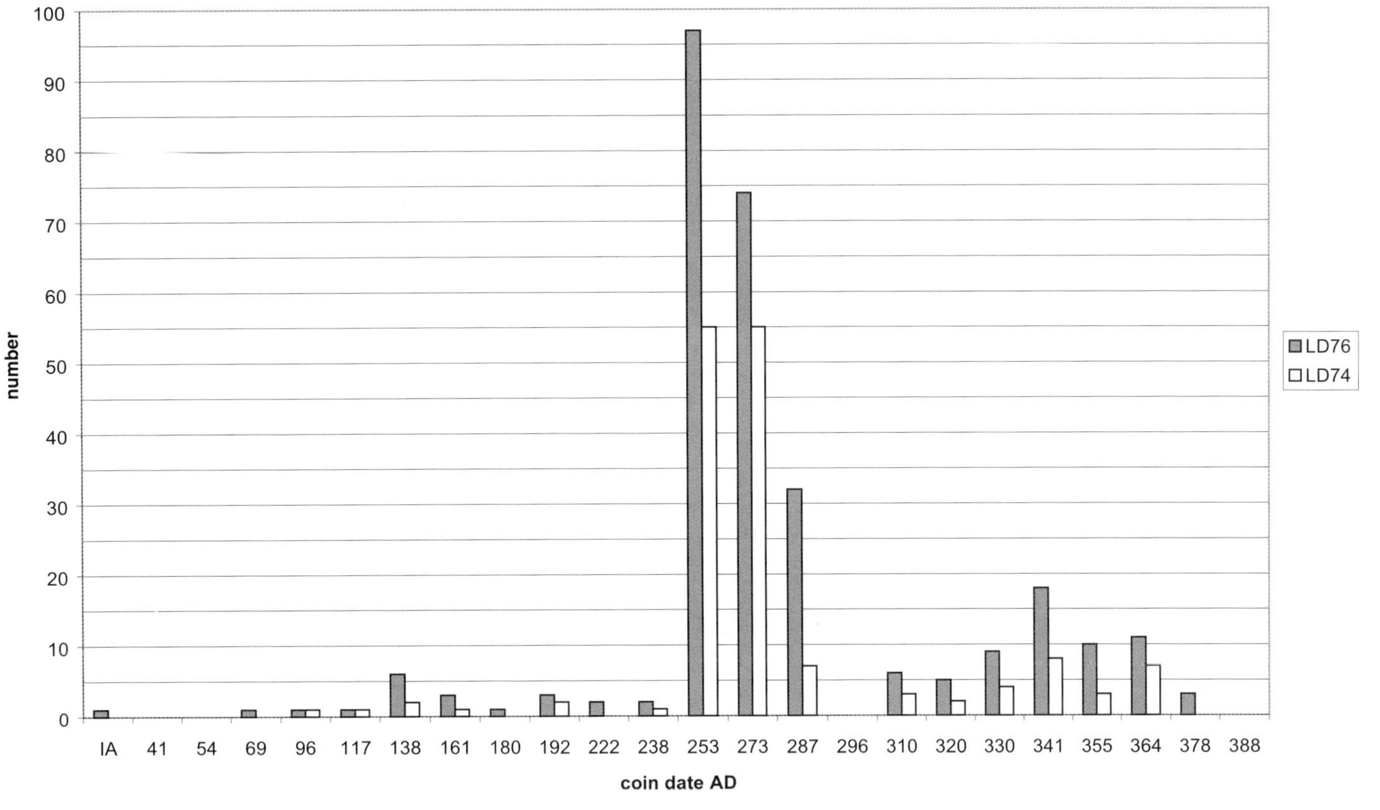

Fig 26 Histogram showing Roman coin distribution at LD76 and LD74

absence of real anomalies, in terms of the presence of late coins in early contexts, might suggest that the interpretation of the limited site records has been carried out with a degree of success.

Distribution of Roman coins between LD74 and LD76

Fig 26 shows the date distribution of the Roman coins found on each site; this exercise has only been carried out in summary form, and not according to contexts, as with Table 14.

As regards the 1st- to 2nd-century coins, upon which it has been observed earlier that all are in a greater or lesser state of wear and hence reached the site at quite a late stage in their lives, 71% were found on LD74. Of the coins from the first half of the 3rd century, 78% were, similarly, from LD74. Of the issues of AD 260–75, 61% are from LD74, and 82% of the coins of Carausius and Allectus are from the same site.

In the 4th century, 70% of the issues of AD 296–330 are from LD74. Of the official issues of AD 330–50, 73% are from LD74, and of the irregular issues of AD 355–65, 70% are. Finally, of the latest issues (AD 364–88), 66% likewise derive from LD74.

In all periods, therefore, the majority of the coins are from LD74, in proportions ranging from 60% to 80%, and predominantly within the range 70–8%. These figures clearly suggest that – unless there was major redistribution of deposits across the site – the greater part of the activity was on LD74 throughout. The closeness with which the histograms reflect each other's pattern also suggests the possibility that activity on each site was a part of the whole, and not necessarily different in nature from that on the other. That is to say whatever was happening on the two Shadwell sites was in fact the same activity, with LD74 nearer to the centre of that activity.

5.7 Leather 'bikini' or briefs

Carol van Driel-Murray

Description

The virtually complete leather garment recovered from a Roman well in Queen Street, London, in 1953 (Wilmott 1982), which has inaccurately, but irrevocably, passed into the literature as a bikini, remained unique until a similar garment was identified amongst the material from the Shadwell excavations. This example differs in several respects from the earlier find, and, by demonstrating the range of variation possible within the general type, provides the key to the identification of at least five further examples, four of them recorded in the MoL archive and ranging in date from the later 1st century (Queen Street) to well into the 4th century (Shadwell and Swan Lane; van Driel-Murray 1999).

Although conventionally described as a bikini, no corresponding leather top has ever been identified and a more accurate description would therefore be leather 'briefs'. The term bikini is, however, now widely accepted and, as will be seen below, it is not inconceivable that cloth bikinis were more common, with leather briefs being used only in specific situations. The Shadwell garment was found, together with a shoe sole (now lost), in the fill of one of the timber-lined tanks (S12, phase 8) which characterise the latest industrial activity on the site. Worn out, discarded clothing can have no relation to the earlier manufacturing activities on the site and the items must be regarded as domestic refuse, dumped in the tanks once they ceased to be utilised. Coins and pottery seem to indicate a date in the middle of the 4th century for the backfill, making the Shadwell example the latest of all the specimens known to date.

The briefs are made of goatskin, and, unlike the Queen Street example, have three integrally-cut laces at each corner, thus requiring a strip of leather at least 450mm long, and probably more as the laces have all snapped during use (Figs 12, 27). In view of its condition, the leather is likely to have shrunk considerably after excavation and some 10–15% should probably be added to the present dimensions. The laces were passed through holes punched in the body of the garment and were tied to give a firm, yet adjustable, cross-over fastening. Deep creases in the leather, the distended lace holes and the distortion around the groin show that the garment was tightly laced, and it is evident that the garment continued to be used even after the original lace holes had become almost entirely useless through excessive wear, since the three strands of the surviving set of ties are still partially knotted with two snapped thongs from the opposite side. Snapping of the ties and, possibly, ripping around the decorative openwork, led to the final discard of the item.

In contrast to the Queen Street bikini, the garment from Shadwell is decorated. The top edge of the back panel is cusped, using a circular punch the same size as that used to make the lace holes. The front panel is decorated with punched-out circles of various sizes, arranged in patterns, now mostly ripped and distorted, but including at least one large circle, triangular arrangements at the ends and smaller circles in between. A perforation visible inside the large circle may have held a metal attachment. Small slit-like (stitch?) holes enclosing the decorated area, and also visible inside the large circle, are suggestive of the attachment of a backing, perhaps of cloth. Though no thread impressions could be discerned, the abraded condition of the leather surface may well mask any traces, and the leather was, moreover, too fragile for an examination of the back (flesh side) to be possible. In general the garment is less well made than the Queen Street example, and in particular lacks the careful edge finishing.

The reconstruction

The garment is too fragile for reshaping to be feasible, but experiments with pliable material suggest that the original shape must have been narrower, while the bowed upper edge is in fact caused by use and the differential shrinkage of the deeply creased areas. On the assumption of symmetry around an axis running from the centre back tab through the crotch and the centre of the largest decorative circle, it is possible to correct the shape and prepare a working model (Fig 27). Although almost nothing remains of the back fastenings, these most probably echoed the arrangement at the front.

Taking account of shrinkage, the hip width of the reconstructed briefs is about 400mm, which on modern criteria would indicate a female wearer aged around 11. However, dimensions recorded from surviving historical costume (Arnold 1985; Bitter 1999) make it abundantly clear that neither modern body measurements, nor the proportions on which modern sizing systems are founded, are particularly relevant to populations in the past. The general impression, from both preserved and excavated clothing, is that people in the past were not so much smaller than now, nor that there has been much change in shoe sizes, but that the differences lay in body mass, with people being thinner and more wiry that is now the case. Measurements taken from children and juveniles at the beginning of this century show marked differences with modern size conventions, especially in female hip and bust measurements. The measurements presented by Martin and Saller (1958) indicate a hip measurement of 300mm for adolescent girls; consequently, the Shadwell briefs could have been worn by a normal, slim, adult woman in the Roman period.

Together with the Queen Street bikini, this new example illustrates the range of variability possible within the basic pattern. Standard appears to be the complex, cross-over lacing through holes in the body of the garment and the hour-glass shape, but the number of laces, their mode of attachment, the presence of decoration and details of size and proportions are variable. In addition to the two, more or less complete specimens, four fragmentary examples have since been identified from London alone, and though further examples probably remain unrecognised in leather collections elsewhere, it is curious that none are present in any of the military complexes familiar to me. The impression from London is that such garments are infrequent, but regularly occurring, items of clothing, strongly associated with civilian and specifically female presence, and being used throughout the entire Roman period. Since at least one fragment has appeared in each major complex of Roman leatherwork from London so far examined, it is evident that leather briefs were by no means uncommon and were discarded together with normal domestic refuse in every area of the city. The smaller population base contributing to military complexes may therefore reduce the statistical chance of finding examples there.

Since Tony Wilmott discussed the available pictorial evidence in relation to the Queen Street bikini it has been generally accepted that these garments were used by semi-nude female acrobats or dancing girls (Wilmott 1982). The earliest reports of the Shadwell example, linking it to a putative military watch tower, only served to reinforce

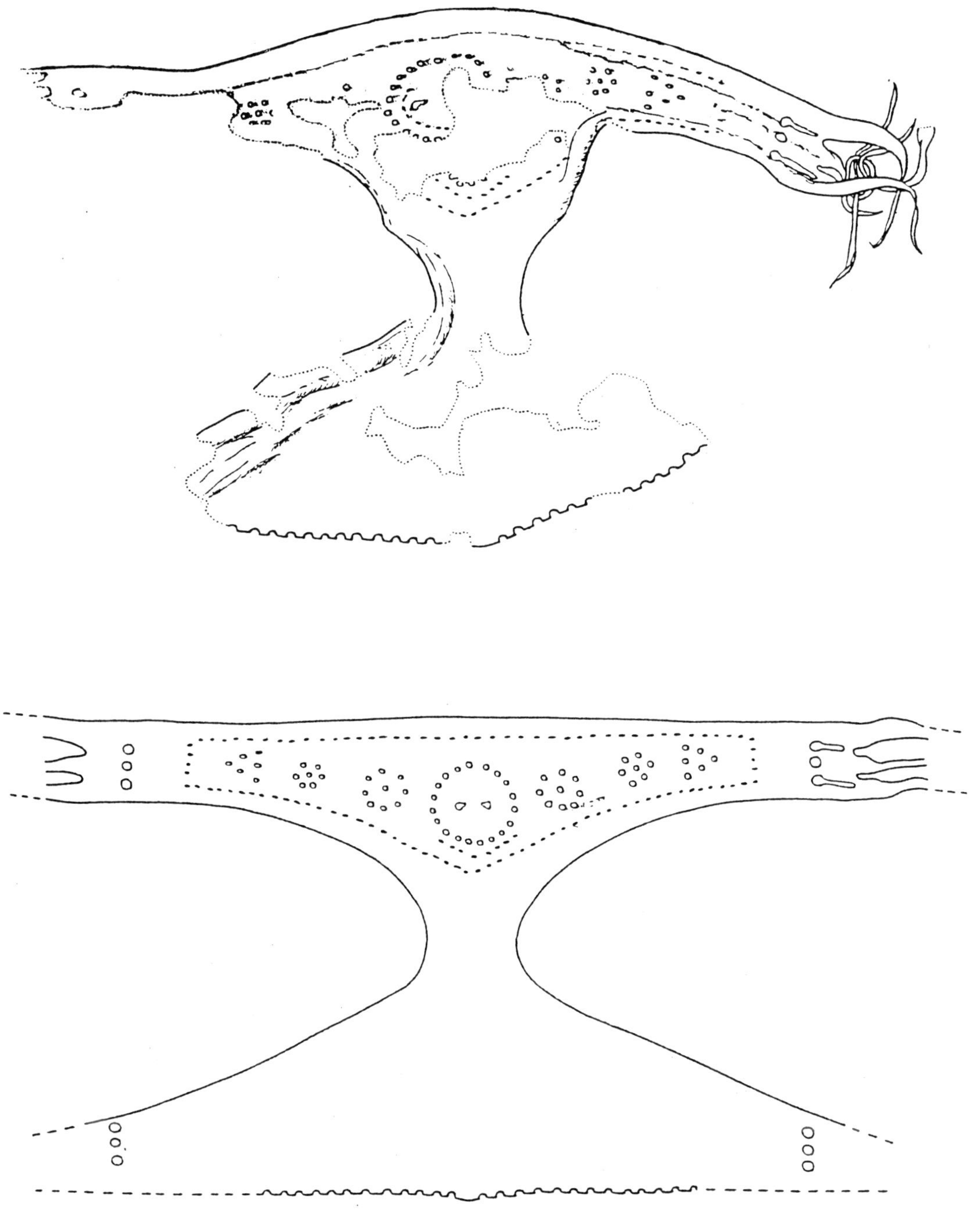

Fig 27 Leather briefs LD74 <383> in present condition and a suggested reconstruction of the original cutting pattern (scale 1:3)

still further the lascivious associations. However, doubts arise when the sheer number of garments and their occurrence amongst mixed domestic refuse is considered: they were evidently being used by quite a wide section of the female population of London. Little is known of female undergarments in the Roman period and though the *subligariorum* of the Vindolanda tablets (Bowman and Thomas 1994, no. 346.4) is generally given as 'underpants' it is not certain whether male of female clothing is concerned, nor what these underpants actually looked like; they could even be the short knee breeches worn by soldiers. The ladies of the Piazza Armerina mosaics are clad in real two-part bikinis, obviously of cloth, but as gymnastic exercises were the only context in which respectable women would be depicted in undress, it may well be that undergarments were more commonly worn, with the briefs occasionally being replaced by leather in particular circumstances. Given the survival rate, and condition when found, of textiles, it is unlikely that an association between cloth upper and leather lower bikini parts will ever come to light, though it needs to be kept in mind. The complex and seemingly excessively firm fastening method of all extant leather examples does invite association with strenuous activity, but any undergarment would need to be secure for daily use. Moreover, the large, almost corset-like examples from Mainz and Swan Lane (London), which reach well up the abdomen, could have served as a supportive garment, while others may have been used to keep wads of textile and moss in place during menstruation. Little is known concerning the practical side of such situations, though in a recent experiment in the Netherlands, where participants attempted to live in a 'prehistoric' manner for two months (in winter!), the women used leather strips for the purpose (Boonstra 1997, 52, fig 18). Unfortunately, the find spot of the Shadwell example, amongst secondarily deposited refuse, where it is clearly an old, worn-out garment, does not shed any new light on the function in detail.

5.8 Animal bone

Kevin Rielly and Charlotte Ainsley

Methodology

All bones were collected by hand. It can therefore be assumed that the bone assemblage will be biased towards the larger animals, for example cattle. This problem arises from the recovery of the more readily visible bones, generally acting against the full recovery of the smaller domesticates such as sheep and pig or the smaller species such as birds and fish.

The animal bones were recorded individually, directly on to the Museum of London Specialist Services (MoLSS) ORACLE database. Identifications of species and anatomy were aided by using the MoLSS reference collections in conjunction with Schmid (1972), and Cohen and Serjeantson (1996). All available information for each bone was recorded, including: proportion present and zones represented (after Rackham 1986); age of the bone (determined through the analysis of tooth wear stages (after Grant 1975) and epiphysial fusion (after Schmid 1972)); butchery, recording cut marks in terms of the tool used, the position of the cut and the direction of the blow; pathology, with a full description and notes taken concerning possible causes; other modifications such as gnawing and burning, in both cases noting the severity, and in the former case, where possible the perpetrator; lastly, measurements, following von den Driesch (1976). The measurements taken were limited to those bones which could be identified as being derived from adult individuals. Where it was impossible to determine exact identifications to species level, approximate classifications based on size were employed, that is 'cattle-sized' and 'sheep-sized'.

Description of the bone assemblage

A total of 1480 fragments (24.00kg) of animal bone were recorded from LD76, of which 745 fragments (18.02kg) of animal bone were selected (on the basis of context date and assemblage size) for further analysis. The selection criteria were met only by assemblages from periods 3 and 5. The species representation for each of the studied periods, by total fragment count and weight with detailed breakdowns by land use, is shown in Table 15, and for cattle alone, by skeletal part in Table 16.

The level of preservation of the bones throughout these deposits would appear to vary between poor and moderate, probably due to poor burial of a proportion of the bones, as well as to soil conditions and their subsequent mixing with other

Table 15 Species representation by period and land use

		Period 3								Period 5			
	Land use	OA5	B1	S4	OA8	S8	S9	Period 3 total	Period 3 total	OA10	OA11	Period 5 total	Period 5 total
Common name	Scientific name	N	N	N	N	N	N	N	Weight (g)	N	N	N	Weight (g)
Cattle	*Bos taurus*	37	0	52	32	11	4	136	6345	109	11	120	4076
Horse	*Equus caballus*	0	1	28	0	2	1	32	2989	4	1	5	142
Cattle-sized		18	1	128	21	21	3	192	2326	29	19	48	608
Sheep/goat	*Ovis/capra* sp	3	1	12	2	3	2	23	124	8	16	24	173
Sheep	*Ovis aries*	1	0	1	0	0	0	2	27	3	2	5	67
Goat	*Capra hircus*	0	0	1	0	0	0	1	5	0	0	0	0
Pig	*Sus scrofa*	1	1	22	4	3	0	31	597	7	8	15	220
Sheep-sized		7	1	29	9	3	1	50	165	6	16	22	66
Dog	*Canis familiaris*	1	0	5	0	0	0	6	46	0	0	0	0
Cat	*Felis domesticus*	0	0	2	1	0	0	3	7	0	0	0	0
Small mammal		1	0	0	0	0	0	1	5	0	0	0	0
Chicken	*Gallus gallus*	3	0	11	1	3	0	18	29.5	0	0	0	0
Chicken-sized		1	0	0	1	0	0	2	2	0	0	0	0
Duck (?domestic)	*Anas* sp	1	0	1	0	1	0	3	7	0	0	0	0
Cod	*Gadus morhua*	0	0	0	0	0	0	0	0	1	0	1	3
Totals		**74**	**5**	**292**	**71**	**47**	**11**	**500**	**12674.5**	**167**	**73**	**240**	**5355**

N is total number of fragments

refuse materials. The level of fragmentation is high; most of it can be related to post-excavation damage, although there is a notably high level of dog-gnawed bones, particularly from the boundary ditch (S4) in period 3 and from period 5 (OA10 and OA11).

Butchery

Most of the observed butchery was found on cattle fragments, a large proportion of which, in both major periods, displayed chop and knife marks. The processes identified are listed below. Additionally, there were a single case of jointing butchery, through the elbow joint, shown by a chopped pig ulna from period 5 (OA10); a dressing cut to a distal chicken tibia from period 3 (S8); and a chop mark to a cod basioccipital from period 5 (OA10) suggesting removal of the head from the remainder of the carcass. The three cases of horse butchery comprise one defleshing cut (period 3, OA5) and two jointing cuts (period 5, OA10 and OA11).

SLAUGHTER

Knife marks visible on the hyoid, although this may also relate to the removal of the tongue; seen in period 3 (S4 and OA8) and period 5 (OA10 and OA11).

SKINNING

Knife marks to a second phalange (period 3 OA5).

DRESSING

Knife cuts to two proximal metatarsal fragments (period 3 OA5); jointing; several cases to the upper limbs and vertebrae, generally chop marks (period 3: OA5, OA8 and S4; period 5: OA10 and OA11).

FILLETING

Or meat removal; again several cases, both chop and knife marks (period 3: OA5, OA8 and S4; period 5: OA10 and OA11).

MARROW EXTRACTION

Split metapodials in period 3 (OA8) and period 5 (OA10).

Age and sex

The cattle age evidence, shown in Tables 17–18, suggests that a major proportion survived into adulthood. This coincides with the third mandibular molar coming into wear and the fusion of the intermediate epiphyses, events occurring at *c* 2 to 2.5 years of age (following Schmid 1972, 75 and 77). There was a cull of young adults (shown by the mandibular third molars with slight wear) which appears to have accounted for a large number of the adults represented in period 5. The final mandible age group may represent animals which were 5 years or older (Maltby, 1981, 182). Unfortunately, given the poor representation of vertebrae in period 5, the epiphysis evidence cannot verify this apparent difference,. Clearly, however, this

Table 16 Cattle skeletal part representation within selected assemblages

Period	3			5
Feature	OA5	S4	OA8	OA10
Carcass part	N	N	N	N
Head and feet	19	16	17	33
Upper limb	6	25	6	33
Lower limb	2	6	0	6
Loose teeth	10	5	9	37
Total bones	**37**	**52**	**32**	**109**

Key to carcass part:-
head and feet: skull, mandible, carpals/tarsals, metapodials and phalanges
upper limb: atlas, axis, scapula, humerus, pelvis and femur
lower limb: radius, ulna and tibia
loose teeth: derived from the maxilla and the mandible, not attributable to an extant tooth row
N is total number of fragments

Table 17 Cattle, sheep/goat and pig mandible toothwear data

Species	Cattle		Sheep/goat		Pig	
Period	3	5	3	5	3	5
Age groups	N	N	N	N	N	N
dpm4w/M1unw	1		1			
M1w/M2unw	2				1	1
M2w/M3unw	2	1	1	2	2	1
M3 slight wear	4	6	1	2	1	
M3 heavy wear	5	2				

Key
N: number of mandibles and/or loose teeth
w: worn
unw: unworn
Age groups:
dpm4: fourth deciduous molar
M1 to M3: adult first to third molars
heavy wear: corresponds to Grant's (1975) stage 'g' or greater for cattle and sheep/goat and 'c' or greater for pigs

Table 18 Epiphysial fusion data

	Cattle		Sheep/goat	Pig	
Period	3	5	5	3	5
Age group	F/UF	F/UF	F/UF	F/UF	F/UF
Neonate	1				
Early	19/0	11/0	5/0	5/0	
Intermediary	8/0	10/0	1/1	1/1	0/2
Late	3/1	5/1	1/0	1/0	1/1
Vertebrae	7/2	1/0			

Key
F: fused
UF: unfused
P: proximal
D: distal
Age groups:-
early: scapula P, humerus D, radius P, pelvis acetabulum and phalange P
intermediary: tibia D, metacarpal D and metatarsal D
late: humerus P, ulna P, radius D, femur P and D, and tibia P
In addition there was one neonate sheep/goat fragment from period 3, Structure 8

evidence does confirm the good survival of young adults, even beyond 3.5 to 4 years (fusion of the late epiphyses), and the abundance of older cattle in period 3 (vertebrae fusing at 7 to 9 years). There are a few very young individuals, even including a neonate plus an infant from period 3. The absence of the younger age groups may be related to preservation biases and poor recovery, rather than to absence based on factors such as preference and/or availability. The evidence for sex (based on the pelves) is very slight, that is, two cows from period 3 and another cow from period 5. As this evidence is based on the pelves, the animals represented may be aged no more than 1 to 1.5 years, corresponding to the fusion of the articulation (the acetabulum) of this skeletal part. With a majority of adult animals, however, it is very likely that these pelves in fact also belong to relatively aged individuals.

Neither the sheep/goat nor pig assemblages provided more than a minor quantity of age evidence. There appears to be a mix of ages, and, in period 5, the majority survived to adulthood, that is about 2 years of age. As with cattle, there is evidence for some stock rearing, demonstrated by the neonate sheep/goat (Table 18) and the infant goat (Table 17) from period 3. Most of the pigs, in both periods, are sub-adult, reflecting the major usage of this species, for its post-mortem products, principally meat.

A large proportion of the chicken bones could be aged, all clearly from adult birds. The sex evidence may indicate a preponderance of hens (four longbones with medullary bone, following Driver 1982), which, in combination with the evidence for adult birds, possibly indicates the importance of egg production.

Finally, a small number of horse and dog bones could be aged. Three horse mandibles, all from period 3 (S4 and S8), featured relatively complete incisor rows. These clearly derived from animals aged (using Goody 1983) 6 to 7 years, 8 years and to a minimum of 15 years. The dog bones were all from adult individuals with the exception of a single fragment with an unfused epiphysis (from period 3, S4), which belonged to an animal no older than 1.5 years of age (Schmid, 1972, 75).

Size

The analysis of size relies on the frequency of particular dimensions taken from bones which are clearly from adult individuals. Amongst the major mammalian domesticates, only cattle provided a reasonable number of the requisite type of measurements, shown in Table 19.

Noticeably, while there is no obvious change in metacarpal size through time, the period 5 metatarsals appear to be smaller than those in period 3. It is conceivable that this difference is merely a reflection of the relatively small datasets. The overall range of sizes conforms to similar measurements taken from a variety of late Roman London sites, for example Baltic House (Table 19; Rielly 2002). This close comparison may also extend to stature, as shown by the withers height of 1177mm calculated from a whole metacarpal (von den Driesch and Boessneck 1974), found in one of the pitfills in period 3 (OA5). In comparison, the range of withers heights from the late Roman Baltic House assemblage was 1068–1178mm with a mean value of 1110mm (n=6).

Table 19 Size of cattle from distal width (Bd) of metapodials

Site	Period	Bone	No.	Range (mm)	Mean (mm)
LD76	3	metacarpal	5	54.2–60.0	55.4
	5	metacarpal	2	54.8–56.4	55.6
	3	metatarsal	2	49.6–63.7	56.6
	5	metatarsal	4	49.1–53.1	51.6
BAX95		metacarpal	10	50.2–74.2	58.6
		metatarsal	6	48.2–65.4	54.4

Measurement (Bd) following von den Driesch (1976)
Baltic House (BAX95) comparisons dated AD 250–400 (Rielly 2002)

A number of the horse bones, while not measurable, could be compared to reference material of known size. They show that horses from this site were similar to middle-sized ponies. This was confirmed by the withers height calculated from a complete metacarpal (from period 3, S4), of 1410mm or 13.8 hands. The noted size range is comparable to that shown elsewhere in Roman London, between 10.8 and 13.75 hands (Rackham 1995, 169).

Conclusions

Period 3

The great majority of the waste bones in this period, as well as in period 5, were clearly derived from food animals. A proportion of these animals, again in both periods, appear to have been reared locally, shown by the likely presence of cattle, sheep/goat and goat infant mortalities. The age evidence is insufficient to allow any clear interpretation of the production status of this settlement, whether most of the meat was supplied or locally produced. There is, however, slight evidence for a local dairy herd, the salient features of which would include the culling of young calves and the survival of relatively aged cows (Legge 1992, 25–6).

The supply of meat clearly involved the importation of whole animals, which would undoubtedly have arrived on the hoof. There is possible evidence for the method of slaughter of cattle, by slitting the throat, and moreover, for the same species, there is evidence for a full range of processing activities, from skinning through to meat removal and marrow extraction. An interesting feature of this butchery is the extensive use of the cleaver, which during this period was apparently a characteristic of urban rather than rural cattle butchery (Maltby 1989, 91). This type of butchery has been linked with the presence of professional butchers, the cleaver being used preferentially to the knife, in an attempt to increase both the speed and efficiency of the butchery process (ibid). Notably, this period did produce concentrations of head and feet parts, from the Open Area 5 pitfills and also the Open Area 8 gullies. These may represent industrial waste, possibly from the supposed tanning activities. However, such waste generally includes concentrations of posterior skull fragments (including the horncores) and foot parts only, these representing the parts which would have been transferred to the tanner still attached to the skin (Serjeantson 1989, 139). The bones from the deposits in question featured a large number of mandibles and very few horncores (see below), probably representing the remains of whole skulls. This type of assemblage is clearly more reminiscent of butchers' waste. The site may therefore have included a butcher, unlike perhaps a typical rural site, where the preparation of carcasses was likely to represent just one of the duties of the local farmer.

The lack of horncores (cattle, as well as sheep and goat) could be the result of their transfer to hornworking establishments. Such workshops were clearly present within Londinium, shown, for example, by the recovery of large concentrations of cattle horncores from 4th-century AD deposits at Angel Court, Walbrook (Clutton-Brock and Armitage 1977, 92).

There is an obviously high proportion of cattle in the period assemblage, as well as within the various features (Tables 15 and 20). The species representation does vary, but this may relate more to the size of the assemblages rather than to actual differences. A high count of cattle is relatively typical for this period, related to the attainment of a widespread preference for beef linked to romanisation, which was originally shown by military, high status and urban centres (King 1984, 193).

There is a notably poor range of other food species, which again may relate to preservation/recovery biases, although these cannot account for the lack of larger game, for example red and roe deer. Chicken would perhaps have been better represented than is indicated by Table 15, and the same may be true of duck. Each of the duck bones is within the size of the wild progenitor, that is mallard, *Anas platyrrhychos*, so these birds may have been either wild or domestic. Chickens were probably kept principally for their eggs, possibly locally, with non-layers inevitably being slaughtered for their meat.

Some of the horses found at this site may have been used for meat. There are two butchered examples, with cuts on bones which are clearly within the meat-rich part of the carcass, and they were in an obvious state of disarticulation. The level of butchery was not, however, comparable to that displayed on the cattle bones, and the horse bones, though highly fragmented, clearly represented larger proportions of skeletal parts (usually at least 50% complete) than did the cattle bones. The great majority of the horse bones are poorly preserved and dog-gnawed, again unlike the cattle fragments, strongly suggesting that these bones

Table 20 Major domesticates by percentage of total fragment count

	Period 3				Period 5		
Land use	OA5	S4	OA8	All	OA10	OA11	All
Species	%	%	%	%	%	%	%
Cattle	57.8	59.0	84.6	71.2	85.8	29.7	76.4
Sheep/goat	16.7	15.9	5.1	13.1	8.7	48.6	18.5
Pig	25.5	25.1	10.3	15.7	5.5	21.7	5.1
Total fragments	**46**	**88**	**39**	**198**	**127**	**37**	**157**

% equals species count/sum of fragments x 100

had been either deposited on the surface or poorly buried. It would perhaps be expected that, if horse were regularly eaten by humans, the bones would show similar characteristics to the cattle fragments. That this is not the case strongly argues for an alternative explanation, possibly the feeding of dogs, which would in turn explain the extensive dog gnawing of and generally poor condition of these bones.

Period 5

This assemblage can be neatly divided into two parts, an earlier phase (OA10) which could conceivably be related to waste items from the preceding industrial phase 8 (period 4) and a later phase (OA11), which, though providing very few bones, is very different from each of the preceding bone groups. The bones from the earlier phase, in common with period 3, are predominantly composed of cattle fragments. There is an even smaller array of species, which may be related to a higher level of fragmentation, possibly to be expected amongst demolition deposits. In common with period 3, there is a distinct lack of cattle horncores, which might suggest the continued practice of sending such raw materials to the hornworker.

The cattle bones within this phase are clearly less aged than those from period 3, with a suggestion of a major cull of young adults. This may demonstrate a change in the local economy away from dairy towards beef production. Obviously this interpretation must remain somewhat tentative due to the small quantities of data.

The abundance of sheep/goat bones within the latest horizons could be indicative of a radical change in local farming practices. This obvious difference must, however, be tempered against the insecure dating evidence.

FRENCH AND GERMAN SUMMARIES

Résumé

Des fouilles ont été entreprises entre 1974 et 1976 dans trois sites (LD74, HIG74 et LD76) situés sur le côté sud de The Highway, Shadwell dans l'arrondissement de Londres de Tower Hamlets. D'importants restes archéologiques des époques romaines et post médiévales ont été trouvées pendant les fouilles y compris la base carrée d'une structure romaine en maçonnerie importante (LD74). A cause de sa forme, de son emplacement et de sa haute visibilité sur la rive nord de la Tamise à environ 1km 25 à l'est du centre de Londinium, le fouilleur l' a interprété comme étant une tour de signalisation de la fin du 3ème siècle. Des structures en bois ont été trouvées à l'est du bâtiment en maçonnerie. L'étude des archives du site a permis une réinterprétation de la chronologie du site qui comprend plusieurs phases d'utilisation allant du 1er à la fin du 4ème siècle.

Le site est situé sur une terrasse de graviers de la Tamise près d'un escarpement important. Les carrières de gravier et d'argile de la fin du 1er et du commencement du 2ème siècle furent remplacées par l'établissement d'un cimetière pour crémations pendant le 2ème siècle comprenant neuf crémations qui ont été relevées en deux groupes. Le site est situé à environ 500m à l'est de l'extrêmité la plus à l'est du cimetière principal situé en dehors de la ville romaine. On pense que la "tour" carrée en maçonnerie mesurant 9m date de la deuxième moitié du 2ème siècle ou légèrement plus tard et que peut-être elle était à la fois contemporaine des crémations et un point focal pour elles. La méthode de construction de la tour avec ses fondations relativement peu profondes est comparable à celle d'un mausolée car l'on pense que certains de ces derniers avaient l'apparence de tours.

Au 3ème siècle, le site fut divisé en deux, d'abord par des clôtures, ensuite par des fossés et des caniveaux et on y construisit un important bâtiment rectangulaire en bois, d'autres structures et des fosses associées à une occupation domestique. Les restes d'animaux retrouvés là indiquent que peut-être des activités de boucherie avaient lieu sur une grande échelle dans les environs immédiats . Au milieu du 4ème siècle, les fossés limitant les champs furent remplis; des citernes doublées de bois et d'argile et des canalisations furent alors construites ce qui indique que l'usage du site devient alors industriel. Une paire de culotte en cuir a été trouvée dans l'une des citernes.

La démolition de la structure en maçonnerie, l'accumulation de matériaux de démolition et celle plus tard de terre agricole marquent l'abandonnement de ce site pendant la seconde moitié du 4ème siècle. Deux inhumations datent aussi peut-être de cette période ce qui indiquerait que le site redevient finalement un cimetière.

La céramique, les pièces de monnaie et les objets en métal de Shadwell sont présents en nombre inhabituellement élevé pour un site non urbain et ont une chronologie peu commune car ils culminent vers la fin du 3ème siècle; il est possible qu'une grande ferme ou un village se trouvait dans les environs. Peu de ces objets ont des caractéristiques militaires. Le site a produit quelques uns des derniers examples de céramique samienne connus émanant de Grande Bretagne et une forte proportion de céramique de l'est de la Gaule tardive.

Zusammenfassung

Die Ausgrabungen fanden zwischen 1974 und 76 an drei Stellen (LD74, HIG74 und LD76) auf der Südseite von The Highway, Shadwell, im Londoner Stadtteil Tower Hamlets statt. Im Laufe der Arbeiten wurden umfangreiche archäologische Überreste aus römischer und nachmittelalterlicher Zeit freigelegt. Dazu gehörte auch das quadratische Fundament eines größeren römischen Mauerwerks (in LD74). Auf Grund seiner Form, Plazierung und Sichtbarkeit am Nordufer der Themse, etwa 1.25km östlich der Hauptsiedlung Londinium, interpretierte der Ausgräber dieses Bauwerk als militärischen Signalturm aus dem späten 3. Jahrhundert. Unmittelbar östlich dieses Bauwerks kamen Holzstrukturen zutage. Der Rückgriff auf das Grabungsarchiv führte zu einer Neuinterpretation der Bebauungsfolge, die nun in mehreren Phasen vom 1. bis ins späte 4. Jahrhundert reicht.

Die Stätte lag auf dem Kies der Uferterrasse der Themse, nahe einer ausgeprägten Uferböschung. Der Kies- und Tonausbeutung während des 1. und frühen 2. Jahrhunderts folgte im 2. Jahrhundert ein Brandbestattungsfriedhof mit neun nachgewiesenen Einäscherungen in zwei Gruppen. Die Ausgrabung liegt etwa 500m östlich der bisher bekannten Ostgrenze des Hauptfriedhofs der römischen Stadt, und 100m südlich der vorgestellten Verlängerung einer römischen Straße, die durch diesen Friedhof führte. Man nimmt jetzt an, daß der 9m im Quadrat gemauerte 'Turm' aus der 2. Hälfte des 2. Jahrhunderts oder aus noch etwas späterer Zeit stammt, und daher gleich alt wie die Begräbnisse und auch deren Mittelpunkt gewesen sein mag. Die Bauweise des 'Turmes' mit seinem relativ flachen Fundament stimmt mit der Bauweise von Mausoleen überein, von denen einige, so nimmt man an, turmartiges Aussehen hatten.

Im 3. Jahrhundert wurde die Gegend zunächst mit Zäunen und dann durch Gräben und Abflußrinnen in Bauplätze eingeteilt. Auch wurden ein größeres, gradliniges Holzgebäude, andere Baustrukturen und Gruben als Zeichen für Besiedlung nachgewiesen. Damit zusammenhängend wurden Tierknochen gefunden, die darauf hindeuten mögen, daß nahebei in großem Ausmaß geschlachtet wurde. Mitte des 4. Jahrhunderts wurde die späteste Phase der Feldeinteilung aufgefüllt und lehm- und holzverkleidete Wasserspeicher und Drainagen errichtet, woraus man schließen mag, daß die Gegend jetzt industriell genutzt wurde. Ein Paar lederne Slips wurden in der Füllung eines der Wasserspeicher gefunden.

Die Zerstörung des Mauerwerks und die Ablagerung zunächst von Bauschutt und später von landwirtschaftlicher Erde zeigen, daß die Gegend in der 2. Hälfte des 4. Jahrhunderts nicht mehr besiedelt war. Zwei Körperbestattungen mögen auch in diese Zeit fallen und auf eine endgültige Rückkehr zur Friedhofsnutzung hindeuten.

Die Ansammlungen von Töpferwaren, Münzen und Metallfunden in Shadwell sind ungewöhnlich groß für eine nichtstädtische Umgebung und haben auch ein ungewöhnliches zeitliches Profil, das seinen Höhepunkt im späten 3. Jahrhundert erreichte. Vielleicht lag hier nahebei ein großer Bauernhof oder eine Hinterlandsiedlung. Die Fundgruppen enthielten wenig, was man als militärisch bezeichnen könnte. Die Grabung lieferte einige der spätesten, in Britannien bekannten Samianfunde mit einem hohen Anteil Spät-Ostgallischer Ware.

BIBLIOGRAPHY

Allason-Jones, L, 1996 *Roman jet in the Yorkshire Museum*, York

Arnold, J, 1985 *Patterns of fashion. The cut and construction of clothes for men and women c 1560–1620*, London

Atkinson, D, 1914 A hoard of samian ware from Pompeii, *J Roman Stud*, 4, 27–64

Baker, J, and Brothwell, D, 1980 *Animal diseases in archaeology*, London

Barber, B, and Bowsher, D, 2000 *The eastern cemetery of Roman London: excavations 1983–90*, MoLAS Monogr Ser 4, London

Barber, B, Bowsher D, and Whittaker, K, 1990 Recent excavations of a cemetery of Londinium, *Britannia* 21, 1–12

Bémont, C, 1977 *Moules de gobelets ornés de la Gaule Centrale au Musée des Antiquités Nationales*, *Gallia* Suppl 33, Paris

Bernhard, H, 1981 Zur Diskussion um die Chronologie Rheinzaberner Relieftöpfer, *Germania*, 59, 79–93

Bird, D, 1996 The London region in the Roman period, in *Interpreting Roman London: papers in memory of Hugh Chapman* (eds J Bird, M Hassall and H Sheldon), Oxbow Monogr 58, 217–32, Oxford

Bird, J, 1986 Samian wares, in Miller, L, Schofield, J, and Rhodes, M, *The Roman quay at St Magnus House, London: excavations at New Fresh Wharf, Lower Thames Street, London 1974–8* (ed T Dyson), London Middlesex Archaeol Soc Spec Pap 8, 139–85

Bird, J, 1987 Two groups of late samian from London, *Rei Cretariae Romanum Fautorum* 25(6), 325–30

Bird, J, 1993 Third-century samian ware in Britain, *J Roman Pottery Stud* 6, 1–14

Bird, J (ed), 1998 *Form and fabric: studies in Rome's material past in honour of B R Hartley*, Oxbow Monogr 80, Oxford

Bird, J, 1999 Decorated Central and East Gaulish samian, in Symonds, R P, and Wade, S, *Roman pottery from excavations in Colchester 1971–86* (eds P Bidwell and A Croom), Colchester Archaeol Rep 10, 75–119, Colchester

Bishop, M C, 1996 *Finds from Roman Aldborough: a catalogue of small finds from the Romano-British town of* Isurium Brigantum, Oxford

Bishop, M C, and Coulston, J C N, 1993 *Roman military equipment*, London

Bitter, P, 1999 *Goed Gevonden: Textielvondsten uit archeologische opgravingen in de Grote of St Laurenskerk te Alkmaar*, Alkmaar

Bittner, F-K, 1986 Zur Forsetzung der Diskussion um die Chronologie der Rheinzaberner Relieftöpfer, *Bayerische Vorgeschichtsblätter* 51, 233–59

Bittner, F-K, 1996 Zur Forsetzung der Diskussion um die Chronologie der Rheinzaberner Relieftöpfer, *Bayerische Vorgeschichtsblätter* 61, 143–74

Boonstra, A, 1997 *Twee manen lang*, Zutphen

Bowman, A K, and Thomas, J D, 1994 *The Vindolanda writing tablets*, London

Brigham, T, 1990 The late Roman waterfront in London, *Britannia* 21, 99–183

Clutton-Brock, J, and Armitage, P L, 1977 Mammal bones from trench A, in Blurton, T R, Excavations at Angel Court, Walbrook, 1974, *Trans London Middlesex Archaeol Soc* 28, 88–97

Cohen, A, and Serjeantson, D, 1996 *A manual for the identification of bird bones from archaeological sites*, London

Crew, P, 1982 *Holyhead mountain Roman watch tower: interim report on the 1980–1 excavations*

Crummy, N, 1983 *The Roman small finds from excavations in Colchester 1971–9*, Colchester Archaeol Rep 2, Colchester

Davies, B J, Richardson, B, and Tomber, R S, 1994 *The archaeology of Roman London: Vol 5, A dated corpus of early Roman pottery from the City of London*, CBA Res Rep 98, York

DGLA, 1989 Department of Greater London Archaeology, London post-excavation review, unpub MoL rep

DUA, 1984 Department of Urban Archaeology, Pottery archive: users handbook, unpub MoL rep

Detsicas, A, 1983 *The Cantiaci*, Gloucester

Dickinson, B M, 1993 The samian ware, in Darling, M J, with Gurney, D, *Caister-on-Sea: excavations by Charles Green, 1951–5*, E Anglian Archaeol Rep 60, 154–60, Gressenhall

Driel-Murray, C van, 1999 'Roman leather bikinis', *Archaeol Leather Grp Newsl* 9, 7–9

Driesch, A von den, 1976 *A guide to the measurement of animal bones from archaeological sites*, Peabody Mus Bull 1, Cambridge Mass

Driesch, A von den, and Boessneck, J A, 1974 Kritische Ammerkungen zur Widerristhöhenberechnung aus Langenmassen vor-und frühgeschichtlicher Tierknochen, *Säugetierkundliche Mitteilungen* 22, 325–48

Driver, J C, 1982 Medullary bone as an indicator of sex in bird remains from archaeological sites, in *Ageing and sexing animal bones from archaeological sites* (eds B Wilson, C Grigson, and S Payne), BAR Brit Ser 109, 251–4, Oxford

Farwell, D E, and Molleson, T I, 1993 *Poundbury: Vol 2, The cemeteries*, Dorset Natur Hist Archaeol Soc Monogr Ser 11, Dorchester

Fletcher, E, and Meates, G W, 1969 The ruined church of Stone-by-Faversham, *Antiq J* 49, 273–94

Fölzer, E, 1913 *Die Bilderschüsseln der ostgallischen Sigillata-Manufakturen*, Rö mische Keramik in Trier 1, Bonn

Frey, M, 1993 *Die Römischen Terra-sigillata-stempel aus Trier*, Trierer Zeitschrift Beiheft 15, Trier

Gard, L, 1937 Reliefsigillata des 3 und 4 Jahrhunderts aus den Werkstätten von Trier, unpub dissertation, Univ Tübingen

Goody, P C, 1983 *Horse anatomy: a pictorial approach to equine structure*, London

Grant, A, 1975 The animal bones, in Cunliffe, B, *Excavations at Portchester castle: Vol 1, Roman*, Rep Res Comm Soc Antiq London 32, 378–408, London

Grimes, W F, 1930 *Holt, Denbighshire: the works-depot of the Twentieth Legion at Castle Lyons*, Y Cwmmrodor 41, London

Hall, J, 1996 The cemeteries of Roman London: a review, in *Interpreting Roman London: papers in memory of Hugh Chapman* (eds J Bird, M Hassall and H Sheldon), Oxbow Monogr 58, 57–84, Oxford

Hammerson, M J, 1978 The coins, in *Southwark excavations 1972–4* (eds J Bird, A H Graham, H L Sheldon and P Townend), London Middlesex Archaeol Soc and Surrey Archaeol Soc Joint Pub 1, London

Hammerson, M J, 1980 Romano-British imitations of the coinage of AD 330–48, unpub MPhil thesis, Univ London

Hammerson, M J, 1996 Problems of Roman coin interpretation in Greater London, in *Interpreting Roman London: papers in memory of Hugh Chapman* (eds J Bird, M Hassall and H Sheldon), Oxbow Monogr 58, 153–64, Oxford

Hammerson, M J, 1997 Roman coins, in Bateman, N, and Porter, G, Guildhall Yard East, EC2, City of London: an archaeological assessment of the excavations over the Roman amphitheatre 1985–97, unpub MoLAS rep

Harden, D B, and Green, C, 1978 A late Roman grave group from the Minories, Aldgate, in *Collectanea Londiniensia: studies in London archaeology and history presented to Ralph Merrifield* (eds J Bird, H Chapman and J Clarke), London Middlesex Archaeol Soc Spec Pap, 163–76, London

Hartley, B R, 1969 The samian pottery, in Wacher, J S, *Excavations at Brough on Humber 1958–61*, Rep Res Comm Soc Antiq London 25, 107–132, London

Henig, M, 1978 *A corpus of engraved gemstones from British sites*, 2 edn, BAR Brit Ser 1, Oxford

Hermet, F, 1934 *La Graufesenque (Condatomago)*, Paris

Hill, J, and Woodger, A, 1999 *Excavations at 72–75 Cheapside/ 83–89 Queen Street, City of London*, MoLAS Archaeol Stud Ser 2, London

Hinton, P, and Thomas, R, 1997 The Greater London publication programme, *Archaeol J* 154, 196–213

Holbrook, N, and Bidwell, P T, 1991 *Roman finds from Exeter*, Exeter Archaeol Rep 4, Exeter

Hornsby, W, and Stanton, R, 1912 The Roman fort at Huntcliff near Saltburn, *J Roman Stud* 2, 215–32

Howe, M D, Perrin, J R, and Mackreth, D F, 1980 *Roman pottery from the Nene Valley: a guide*, Peterborough City Museum Occas Pap 2, Peterborough

Huld-Zetsche, I, 1971 Glatte Sigillaten des 'Massenfundes' aus Trier, *Rei Cretariae Romanae Fautorum Acta* 13, 21–39

Huld-Zetsche, I, 1972 *Trierer Reliefsigillata: Werkstatt I*, Materialen zur römisch-germanischen Keramik 9, Bonn

Huld-Zetsche, I, 1998 Zur Verwertbarkeit von Reliefsigillaten des 2 und 3 Jahrhunderts, in Bird, 147–9

Hull, M R, 1963 *The Roman potters' kilns of Colchester*, Rep Res Comm Soc Antiq London 21, London

Isings, C, 1957 *Roman glass from dated finds*, Groningen

Jessup, R F, 1959 Barrows and walled cemeteries in Roman Britain, *J Brit Archaeol Ass* 22, 1–32

Johnson, A, 1977 The Roman watchtower at Shadwell, London, unpub BA dissertation, Univ Wales

Johnson, T, 1975 A Roman signal-tower at Shadwell, E1; an interim note, *Trans London Middlesex Archaeol Soc* 26, 278–80

King, A C, 1984 Animal bones and the dietary identity of military and civilian groups in Roman Britain, Germany and Gaul, in *Military and civilian in Roman Britain: cultural relationships in a frontier province* (eds T C Blagg and A C King), BAR Brit Ser 136, 187–218, Oxford

Kortüm, K, and Mees, A, 1998 Die Datierung der Rheinzaberner Reliefsigillata, in Bird, 157–68

Lawson, A, 1975 Shale and jet objects from Silchester, *Archaeologia* 105, 241–75

Legge, A J, 1992 *Excavations at Grimes Graves, Norfolk: 4, Animals, environment and the Bronze Age economy*, London

Ludowici, W, 1927 *Stempel-Namen und Bilder römischer Töpfer, Legions-Ziegel-Stempel, Formen von Sigillata und anderen Gefässen aus meinen Ausgrabungen in Rheinzabern 1901–14*, Munich

Ludowici, W, and Ricken, H (eds), 1948 *Katalog VI meiner Ausgrabungen in Rheinzabern 1901–14: Die Bilderschüsseln der römischen Töpfer von Rheinzabern, Tafelband*, Speyer

Lyne, M A B, and Jefferies, R S, 1979 *The Alice Holt/Farnham Roman pottery industry*, CBA Res Rep 30, London

McIsaac, W, Schwab, I, and Sheldon, H, 1979 Excavations at Old Ford, 1972–5, *Trans London Middlesex Archaeol Soc* 30, 39–96

Mack, R P, 1975 *The coinage of Iron Age Britain*, 3 edn, London

Mackinder, A, 2000 *A Romano-British cemetery on Watling Street: excavations at 165 Great Dover Street, Southwark, London*, MoLAS Archaeol Stud Ser 4, London

Maltby, M, 1981 Iron Age, Romano-British and Anglo-Saxon animal husbandry – a review of the faunal evidence, in *The environment of man: the Iron Age to the Anglo-Saxon period* (eds M Jones and G Dimbleby), BAR Brit Ser 87, 155–203, Oxford

Maltby, M, 1989 Urban rural variations in the butchering of cattle in Romano-British Hampshire, in *Diet and crafts in towns* (eds D Serjeantson and T Waldron), BAR Brit Ser 199, 75–106, Oxford

Marsh, G, 1981 London's samian supply and its relationship to the development of the Gallic samian industry, in *Roman pottery research in Britain and north-west Europe: papers presented to Graham Webster* (eds A C Anderson and A S Anderson), BAR Int Ser 13, 173–238, Oxford

Marsh, G, and Tyers, P, 1979 The Roman pottery from Southwark, in *Southwark excavations 1972–4* (eds J Bird, A H Graham, H L Sheldon and P Townend), London Middlesex Archaeol Soc and Surrey Archaeol Soc Joint Pub 1, 533–82, London

Martin, R, and Saller, K, 1958 *Lehrbuch der Anthropologie*, 3 edn, Stuttgart

Mattingly, H, Sydenham, E A, et al (eds), 1923–94 *The Roman imperial coinage*, 10 vols, London

May, T, 1916 *The pottery found at Silchester*, Reading

Mees, A, 1993 Zur Gruppenbildung Rheinzaberner Modelhersteller und Ausformer, *Jahresbericht aus Augst und Kaiseraugst* 14, 227–55

Mees, A, 1994 Potiers et moulistes: observations sur la chronologie, les structures et la commercialisation des ateliers de terre sigillée décorée, in *Actes du Congrès de Millau, 12–15 mai 1994, Société Française d'Étude de la Céramique Antique en Gaule*, 19–41, Marseille

Merrifield, R, 1983 *London: city of the Romans*, London

Nash-Williams, V E, 1930 The samian potters' stamps found at Caerwent (*Venta Silurum*) in Monmouthshire, *Bull Board Celt Stud* 5, 166–85

Oelmann, F, 1914 *Die Keramik des Kastells Niederbieber*, Materialen zur römisch-germanischen Keramik 1, Frankfurt am Main

Oswald, F, 1936–7 Index of figure-types on terra sigillata ('samian ware'), *Annals Archaeol Anthropol* 23, 1–4, and 24, 1–4, Liverpool

Oswald, F, 1945 Decorated ware from Lavoye, *J Roman Stud* 35, 49–57

Oswald, F, and Pryce, T D, 1920 *An introduction to the study of terra sigillata, treated from a chronological standpoint*, London

Ottaway, P, 1995 *Romans on the Yorkshire coast*, York

Perrin, J R, 1999 Roman pottery from excavations at and near to the Roman small town of *Durobrivae*, Water Newton, Cambridgeshire, 1956–8, *J Roman Pottery Stud* 8

Petrikovits, H von, 1971 Fortifications in the north-western Roman Empire from the third to the fifth centuries AD, *J Roman Stud* 61, 178–218

Price, J, 1979 The glass, in Frocester Court Roman villa, second report 1968–77: the courtyard (eds H S Gracie and E G Price), *Trans Bristol Gloucestershire Archaeol Soc* 97, 9–64

Rackham, D J, 1986 Assessing the relative frequency of species by the application of a stochastic model to a zooarchaeological database, in *Database management and zooarchaeology*(ed L H van Wijngaarden-Bakker), *PACT (J European Study Grp Physical, Chemical, Biological Mathematical Techniques applied to Archaeology)* Res Vol 40, 185–92, Amsterdam

Rackham, D J, 1995 Skeletal evidence of medieval horses from London sites, in *The medieval horse and its equipment c 1150–1450* (ed J Clark), HMSO Medieval Finds from Excavations in London Ser 5, 169–74, London

Reutti, F, 1983 Tonverarbeitende Industrie im römischen Rheinzabern, *Germania* 61, 33–69

Richardson, B, 1986 Pottery in Miller, L, Schofield, J, and Rhodes, M, *The Roman quay at St Magnus House, London: excavations at New Fresh Wharf, Lower Thames Street, London 1974–8* (ed T Dyson), London Middlesex Archaeol Soc Spec Pap 8, 96–138

Ricken, H, 1934 Die Bilderschüsseln der Kastelle Saalburg und Zugmantel, *Saalburg Jahrb* 8, 130–82

Ricken, H, and Fischer, C (eds), 1963 *Die Bilderschüsseln der römischen Töpfer von Rheinzabern: Textband mit Typenbildern zu Katalog VI der Ausgrabungen von Wilhelm Ludowici in Rheinzabern 1901–1914*, Materialen zur römisch-germanischen Keramik 7, Bonn

Rielly, K, 2002 The animal bones, in Howe, E, *Roman defences and medieval industry: excavations at Baltic House, City of London*, MoLAS Monogr Ser 7, 94–104, London

Rogers, G B, 1974 *Poteries sigillées de la Gaule Centrale: I, Les motifs non figurés*, *Gallia* Suppl 28, Paris

Serjeantson, D, 1989 Animal remains and the tanning trade, in *Diet and crafts in towns* (eds D Serjeantson and T Waldron), BAR Brit Ser 199, 129–46, Oxford

Schmid, E, 1972 *Atlas of animal bones*, London

Schulz, R, and Schellenberger, W, 1996 *Museumskatalog Terra-Sigillata in Rheinzabern*, Terra-Sigillata-Museum Rheinzabern

Seeley, F, 2000 The Roman pottery, in Mackinder, 53–7

Seeley, F, in prep The Roman pottery, in Cowan, C, Wheeler, L, and Westman A, *Roman Southwark: origins, development and economy*, MoLAS Monogr Ser, London

Sheldon, H, 1972 Excavations at Parnell Road and Appian

Road, Old Ford E3, February–April 1971, *Trans London Middlesex Archaeol Soc* 2, 101–47

Sheldon, H, and Yule, B, 1979 Excavations in Greenwich Park 1978–9, *London Archaeol* 3, 311–17

Simon, H-G, 1968 Das Kleinkastell Degerfeld in Butzbach, Kr Friedberg (Hessen): Datierung und Funde, *Saalburg Jahrb* 25, 5–27

Simon, H-G, and Köhler, H-J, 1992 *Ein Geschirrdepot des 3 Jahrhunderts: Grabungen im Lagerdorf des Kastells Langenhain*, Materialen zur römisch-germanischen Keramik 11, Bonn

Simpson, G, 1976 Decorated terra sigillata at Montans (Tarn) from the manuscript of Elie Rossignol at Albi, *Britannia* 7, 244–73

Stanfield, J A, and Simpson, G, 1958 *Central Gaulish potters*, London

Symonds, R P, 2000 Burial goods and pottery cremation urns, in Barber and Bowsher, 117–41

Symonds, R P, and Tomber, R S, 1991 Late Roman London: an assessment of the ceramic evidence from the City of London, *Trans London Middlesex Archaeol Soc* 42, 59–99

Tilhard, J-L, 1998 Un vase moulé de Montans au décor volontairement effacé, in Bird, 123–5

Ward, M, 1993 A summary of the samian ware from excavations at Piercebridge, *J Roman Pottery Stud* 6, 15–22

Wardle, A, in prep The Roman finds, in Cowan, C, *Urban development in north-west Roman Southwark: excavations 1974–90*, MoLAS Monogr Ser, London

Wilmott, T, 1982 Excavations at Queen Street and Roman wells in London, *Trans London Middlesex Archaeol Soc* 33, 1–78

Young, C J, 1977 *Oxfordshire Roman pottery*, BAR Brit Ser 43, Oxford

Zadoks-Josephus Jitta, A N, Peters, W J T, and Witteveen, A, 1973 *Description of the collections in the Rijksmuseum G M Kam at Nijmegen: VII, The figural bronzes*, Amsterdam

INDEX

Compiled by Susanne Atkin

Page numbers in **bold** refer to illustrations